WHEN
LOVERS
ATTACK

How to Stop
Fighting
and Get
Back to Sex

SEVA KENN

First published by Seva Media in 2019

DISCLAIMER: The information contained in this book is a reflection
of the author's personal and professional experiences, and therefore
does not apply to all persons, or to all situations. The reader must
judge the appropriateness, usefulness, or safety of any idea, sugestion,
recommendation, or practice described. The author and publisher dis-
claim any and all liability for any adverse effects resulting directly or
indirectly from information contained in this book.

Editor: Richard Willett and ProWritingAid
Cover design: pro_ebookcovers

ISBN 978-1-7336770-0-4

First edition

Contents

Acknowledgements

My children, who taught me so much about myself.

LM, who introduced me to emotional expression via the concepts of Re-evaluation Counseling.

Julie, who welcomed me so fully.

The market crash of 2008, which forced me to find a new career.

Desert Nichols, for his contributions to the field of sexual healing.

Cheryl, who so diligently healed herself, then shared her inborn sexual power with me. And mastered my communication teachings.

Kamala Devi McClure and her 2016 writers' group.

Robin Harris and the Sedona Library writers' group.

Introduction

On a hot day, I am enticed by convenience store displays of Monster, Rock Star, or any new hydration product. Health conscious decision-making goes out the window when my throat is dry and my energy is low.

But my partner and travel mate never wavers. Only naturally flavored teas for her. Cheryl is attractive and emotionally intelligent, but in my view, overly purist.

As I study a Red Bull Sugarfree label, Cheryl's opinions on artificial ingredients interrupt my chemical discovery enthusiasm. The intrusion is unwelcome. Adrenaline ripples my stomach and furrows my brow, as if a salesperson were trying to close on me. I act like nothing has happened when I return to the car with a neon-blue G2 Thirst Quencher.

Raising the bottle to my lips, I symbolically reject Cheryl the product safety monitor. She has the impulse to say something. Her eyes gawk at the glowing liquid, then away. Her jaw tightens. Her beliefs about artificial coloring are so strong, she can't control her observable reactions.

In lockstep, I react to her reactions. That Cheryl is not joyful as I take my first gulp, makes me mad. My primal self hates any resistance to its fun or freedom. Sensations of displeasure increase. I want her gone.

Time slows down as we register the bothersome impasse, and contemplate a way out. Cheryl makes the first move, trying to sound neutral. "That is an unusually bright color."

"Yes," I admit, nestling the bottle into the console cup holder. I want to say more, but wait for a flicker of inspiration. "That's what makes it fun!" I smile broadly in self amusement, then we both laugh, welcoming any excuse to rejoin our good natures.

Moments of conflict with a lover are intense, regardless the gravity of content. If I am paying attention, I will notice a millisecond of blind rage surge through my body when I see Cheryl's look of disapproval. It's a hair trigger, like road rage, but I don't yell or pound on the steering wheel.

I remind myself to be civilized when Cheryl hopes to cut off my beverage-independence manhood. But panic symptoms go deeper than any of my philosophies. For a second I am simply a primate protecting its turf.

That is a very important second, which can rapidly fork into infinite lines of overt or covert escalation. How to handle unsettling hormone spikes, and the thoughts and emotions they produce, is the essence of my coaching practice.

Instinctive impulses need to be reset. All lovers become more sensitive as sexual chemistry dials back to a long-term baseline. Disagreements, disappointments, and disparities of every size and shape, take on greater significance, and seldom conclude with a laugh or a hug.

The unresolved drips of irritation steadily fill a bucket of resentment. Then along comes a nudge to hurl the bucket. Unprocessed angst catches up with the present. Out comes a dis, a rebuke, a verbal blow. The target is shocked, but instinctively fires back, or withdraws into a protective shell.

It's unsettling when the person who matters most turns on you. Even if the jab is subtle and confusing, an internal alarm goes off. I call it what it feels like: An attack.

An attack of any scale, physical, mental, or emotional, is the opposite of funny, because some part of us gets damaged. I in no way wish to discourage unruly banter. If your lover is laughing, great. But if not, something may have hurt.

In my observation, no couple escapes hurtful interactions. And no one knows what to do when that happens. I certainly didn't when I was younger.

I would have taken Cheryl's blue-dye disgust seriously. "She's always bringing me down!" I might have thought, obliterating the positive, even ecstatic feelings I have for her.

Or I could have interpreted her "bright color" statement as an indictment of my character, instead of just a fact. Fortunately, I have trained myself to slow down and parse my reactions. To wait for a non-defensive perspective.

It took zero effort to say "Yes" to Cheryl's opening line. To validate the truth of her words. Arguing that the color was *not* bright would have trapped me as surely as a power winch tightening my seatbelt.

Then I shared my truth. Playfully, but with a slight edge. Enough to satisfy me, but not provoke. Cheryl helped by choosing a re-connection fork, allowing herself to be warmed by my smile. Practice has enabled us to direct ourselves to the smidgeon of effort that reaps a mountain of reward.

I resisted that smidgeon of effort as much as anyone, but finally realized that fighting with a lover is too depressing. That's when a better way presented itself. Over the course of two decades I mastered several counseling methodologies, adapted them to the rigors of relationship life, and observed their effectiveness in personal and professional real-time.

How effective? The methods described in this book are 1,440 times more effective than doing nothing, or something desperate. No kidding.

Conflicts dissipate, to varying degrees, by ignoring them, trying to forget them, or attempting but failing to resolve them. That takes, let's say, three days, or 4,320 minutes, until a tentative friendliness returns.

But *effective* behavior can turn a conflict into a connection in as little as three minutes. The ratio of three minutes to 4,320 minutes is, yep, one to 1,440. This enormous savings is not only in time, but vitally, in reduced injury to quality-of-life.

Extended animosity is harmful to lover relationships. In the words of Anais Nin, "Love... dies of weariness, of witherings, of tarnishings."

The need to de-escalate is *urgent* when lovers divide into opposing forces. Before the gauntlet is thrown and swords are drawn.

1

Sexual Frustration

Falling in love is a priceless gift to us from nature, but it is not free. Under the influence of limitless love and peaks of pleasure, we career into unscripted relationships. In our giddiness, we ignore downside outcomes.

An outcome we don't see coming is crashing from the being-in-love high. Whether it happens slowly or swiftly, coming down is unnerving. Fear creeps in to the pit of the stomach. We become cranky and paranoid. At that point, we are a danger to ourselves, and to the person we so recently loved and cherished.

Hopefully, you will never face an angry lover armed with a samurai sword. But hurtful words that cut to your core are almost a certainty. Even if a lover's words were not intentionally harmful, an invisible blade hits its mark. Your body reacts likes it's wounded and bleeding. You feel faint, awkward, incompetent, and hopeless.

Your lover said something, and your interior self tanked. Out of habit or willpower, you remain standing, but your mood has sunk to the floor. Tanking, or triggering, as described in Chapter 6, is an involuntary reflex. The limbic system of your brain—which processes fear and mediates the fight-or-flight response—took over. It made you react, like ducking from a loud bang.

Most people do not take an engine backfire from across the street as a personal affront, as if the car were purposefully trying to injure their eardrums. But it's a different story when humans backfire. Imagine that a couple is getting ready to go out for drinks. Lover A wants to look good in public, so makes a comment.

Lover A: "That shirt is dirty."

Lover B: "I don't give a fuck!"

Whoa! Where did that come from? Lover B's reply is like the whole engine blowing up. It shocks the nervous system of both partners. For some reason, Lover B interpreted the shirt comment as a smack down. It was perceived as a personal attack, instead of just information about the evening's dress code. Perhaps Lover B had become traumatized by Lover A's perfectionism.

For whatever reason, Lover B's limbic system took over and defended against the perceived attack. The limbic system is programmed to ensure survival. It is our inner warrior and takes action without permission. Threats then get handled before thinking can intervene.

A quick reaction to threats is good for survival. But the instrument is blunt. It does not easily distinguish between a real threat, like a car veering into your lane, and a perceived threat, like "that shirt is dirty."

How is it possible to react so uncontrollably to a statement? Dramatic reactions don't come out of nowhere. A specific set of hurts have gone untended. Snarling is an attempt to bring the problem to the surface.

In the above scenario, the words "I don't give a fuck!" are an obvious jab at Lover A. The phrase could mean that Lover B has "had it" with Lover A's comments, or it could mean Lover B has given up on the relationship. However deep the meaning is, it is mood injuring to Lover A. Lover A feels attacked.

But who attacked first? Lover B would say the shirt comment came first. Lover B felt attacked because genuine effort was put into picking an appropriate shirt. Lover A then feels attacked by Lover B's outrage. A fight ensues.

What is an Attack?

An attack is anything you don't like on a visceral level. That upsets your innards. That slips past your rational or conscious mind and wreaks havoc on your equanimity. One moment you are clicking along, enjoying your flow, and the next moment, you are not.

You may be suddenly self-conscious, nervous, or flustered, as bodily sensations interfere with thinking. You are caught off guard. Muscles stiffen up and movement is awkward. You might be at a loss for words and feeling trapped.

Something happened to you too fast to stop. Your peace or happiness got whacked. The "good" you was strangled and it happened when you were interacting with your lover. An easy conclusion is that your lover "caused" it. The real situation is more nuanced.

For example: Let's say your lover once had a traumatizing oral sex experience and "tanks," shuts down, or gets cranky whenever you express interest in giving your love orally. Your lover can't control this reaction, and will feel attacked (pressured), regardless of your heartfelt presentation. A snappish rebuff to your sweetness makes *you* feel attacked. Yikes! The trail of cause and effect can be hard to follow.

Couples don't budget time to unearth the true causes and effects of their behavior. And there honestly may not be enough time. They need shortcuts. One useful shortcut is to accept that one of you will feel attacked at some point, that a strong reaction may result, and it is not the end of the world.

Everyone has sensitivities, so feeling attacked, and reacting to that feeling, is going to happen. What occurs *next* is the important part. Because our primate behaviors are so observable, it is essential to increase awareness of them, to moderate their effect.

Each side of a dyad depends on the other for the smoothest possible functioning, and that takes effort. Both partners may try not to sink from small attacks.

Reaction control is effective enough that most attacks slip under the defense radar. But the limbic system records them, and stores them in memory. Because so many attacks appear to slip under the radar, people act as if they have *no* effect, encouraging a divide between public behaviors and private thoughts. But those private thoughts are important.

Products of our brains, such as thoughts, feelings, and behaviors, pop into being like antimatter, and affect the present of ourselves and our lover. We don't have control over what arises in our minds. There is no social obligation for guilt or shame. But we can control what happens next.

A rocky internal landscape affects your lover whether you want it to or not. There doesn't seem to be a pause button you can push to give you the years it might take to fix all your weaknesses. In spite of that, your lover has come to expect your best behavior.

Once you fall in love, relationship is "live" until, or if, there is a breakup. You are onstage, and your lover is the audience. That may be too much responsibility for some people, causing them to act out, or bail.

If thoughts, feelings, and actions arise unbidden from the subconscious, why should we be held responsible for any consequences? Good question! I believe the path of greatest responsibility is the most successful, empowered, and satisfying. If we accept responsibility for what we do *next*, then we are not slaves to our own subconscious disturbances, or those of our lovers.

We will never escape our rocky internal landscape, our feelings of being attacked, and our limbic system's blunt instruments, but we can learn to recognize all of those states within ourselves, and guide our behavior towards less damaging consequences. So we can salvage the dicey moment before we bludgeon our partner with a negativity club. Before the spark between us goes out.

Attacks Affect Sexiness

In the beginning, positivity flows out of us in a torrent. We juice each other to a degree that appears ridiculous to outside observers. Hence the phrase "sickeningly in love." But over-the-top positivity is normal to lovers, whose brains are flooded with dopamine, a neurotransmitter that mediates desire and motivation.

As dopamine production dwindles, positivity is less rewarding. Juice from the "dark side" fills the gap, inducing the urge to "fuck with" each other. As normal as that urge may be, fucking with a lover catches the attention of the limbic system's safety regulator, which gradually dials down the chemistry of sexual arousal. We are literally on the brink of choosing to "fuck with" instead of fuck.

The whole history of the relationship affects the mechanisms of genital blood flow. The capillaries of erectile tissue are not opened through sheer willpower. It takes the cooperation of the limbic system. The same system that never stops evaluating safety based on the number of recorded hurts.

As the number of hurts stack up—stimulating production of the stress hormone cortisol—*problems* with having sex slowly become more noticeable than pleasures. The frequency of sex then decreases, along with the pleasure that can be felt when sex happens.

Sex becomes a question mark, instead of a given. When will it happen? How will it be initiated? Will it feel good? This is the state of sexual frustration. Attempts to initiate sex are not successful. Confidence erodes, leading to a discouraging cycle of failure. The body's primal need for sex is not fulfilled, increasing anxiety, which puts pressure on the need to have sex. Increased pressure and anxiety create a higher barrier to having sex, resulting in even less sex.

This is a giant conundrum! Something that could soothe the limbic system, sex, does not get to do its job. Sex is not just one of those things that couples do along with conversation, dinner, and house renovations. Sex is a significant signal to the limbic system regarding the overall health of the relationship. If having sex is not satisfying or soothing, then dark-side juice gets tastier.

Soothing sex tells the limbic system that everything is OK. Lack of soothing sex does the opposite. Reactions to this discomfort cannot be suppressed or controlled. The need for sexual fulfillment is too primal. In spite of honorable intentions, sexual frustration often leads to flirtation with non-partners and infidelity.

As the being-in-love state wears off, we are left with a challenging cocktail of increased sensitivities, less confidence, less certainty, and less sexual satisfaction to miraculously fix everything. The table below lists some symptoms of being in love, compared to the after-peak period.

In-Love Condition	After Peak Symptoms
Giddy High	Coming Down From High
Minimized Needs	Needs Reset to Normal
Best Behavior	Average Behavior
Needs Easily Met	Meeting Needs Takes Effort
High Interest and Caring	Caring Requires Focus
Ego Reduced	Ego Reasserts Itself
Confidence Is Boosted	Challenges to Confidence
Sexual Certainty	Sexual Frustration
Openness and Oneness	Guarded and Isolated
Generous	Concern for Fairness
All Is Good	Some Good, Some Bad
Safe and Supported	Not Fully Safe
Togetherness Is Comforting	Time Apart Is Comforting
Quirks Are Adorable	Quirks Are Irritating
Single Lover Focus	Desire Starts to Stray
Positivity Is Automatic	Positivity Requires Skills

The transition to after-peak is practically universal, so it is probably a natural part of human biology. If it can't be stopped, then all we can do is make the best of it. This unwanted gift of bumps and bruises can be utilized as a consistent opportunity for personal growth.

Perspectives on Frustration

Familiarity can reduce anxiety and fear. Most of us partake in other biochemical activities, such as drinking beer or wine, competing in a sport, or gorging on a special meal. Beforehand, we might even feel a powerful "jones" for that activity. Although we choose to not think of the consequences, we understand and sometimes laugh about hangovers, sore muscles, and bloating. The predictable stages of irresistible desire, fulfillment, and crash back to baseline don't stop us from repeating activities we are voluntarily into. Living through the downside doesn't unhinge us.

I propose that it is equally possible to normalize the symptoms of coming down from the being-in-love binge. It would be nice to get comfort and wisdom from our lovers in dealing with the symptoms, but our lovers have the same symptoms, and also need help.

Both lovers become more sensitive, less well behaved, and inclined again to care more about their individual selves. And they both want the other one to continue with in-love joyfulness and sexual abandon. They want to keep their fantasy lover. When reality intrudes on fantasy, the rudeness of the interruption is shocking. It is resisted. And it is resented.

When boosting switches to testing, when support switches to questioning, when sex is frustrating instead of automatic, lovers no longer feel as safe with each other. Less safe to be silly, controversial, experimental, expressive, giving, and revealing. It becomes harder to be good and do good. The belief that "we're in this together" returns to "I need to take care of myself." Invincibility morphs into vulnerability.

It is frightening when your heart and body are no longer held in exquisite reverence. Reverence, respect, and regard allowed you to be your most amazing self. That self felt so good! The sacred altar of love is replaced by a cutting board, with your lover cutting you down to size.

If the heart and body are no longer safely held, the limbic system treats that as a threat, and takes steps to reverse vulnerability. The erosion of being in love has begun.

Openness and easy sexual attraction are taken for granted at first. Dopamine hops over relationship obstacles as if they weren't there. But too soon, obstacles become visible, and conflict overshadows safety and ease.

Marriage and commitment are attempts to solve this devolution. But security is not the same as safety. Legal and financial entanglements raise the exit bar, and that can lengthen the time couples stay in physical proximity. But that does not reduce infidelity, or keep sex alive.

The problem is, marriage does not guarantee the quality of partner interaction. Safety is the ultimate state that feels good emotionally and physically, and motivates continuation. There is nothing better. The giving and receiving of safety stimulates love, defuses conflicts, and heals wounds.

Alert: Safe behavior can be learned.

When communication and commitment break down, when suitability for each other is an open question, when sex isn't automatic—as in effortlessly turned on, can barely stop ourselves from having sex—we can learn to take that in as important information, instead of highlighting it as something that is "wrong."

Our egos love the word wrong, since it infers a problem coming from outside ourselves. This is a simplistic first line of ego defense. The ego likes to shift blame elsewhere. That elsewhere is our lover.

We think something is wrong when lovers exhibit after-peak symptoms. We think they are maliciously withdrawing their sexual allure and tender loving. The truth is, nature is to blame. Nature evolved our biochemistry, which pushes us into arrangements that are over our heads.

Our inclination is to revere a lover for making us feel so magnificent, then hate that same lover when they stop. You thought it was your lover who was making you feel so good, but it was really your own biochemistry. I offer as proof the human ability to fall in love with a movie or TV character. Nothing has happened other than light went into eyes and sound went into ears, yet voilà!

A fundamental biochemical change happened within your imagination via the tricks of screenwriting, directing, and acting. You didn't have to do anything except buy a ticket. Your body was designed to do the rest. Movie owners, distributors, and theaters are not held accountable for pulling audiences' heartstrings. Award-winning acts of love and productions of pleasure by partners can be viewed the same way.

The fall into love is a scene that has already been written. It is just waiting for the green light on sex. For the eruption of desire to override discipline. The sensation of desire is not controlled by the mind, by the will. We can place ourselves in settings that encourage attraction and desire, and endure settings that discourage it. But the sensation itself, which motivates behavior, is not under our control.

When the sensation of attraction and desire is felt, behavior is motivated toward sex. When that sensation is not felt, behavior toward sex is not motivated. It's that simple. When one partner loses attraction and becomes unmotivated, or both partners do, it can be sad, and possibly maddening, if there appears to be no reason for it.

It may be hard to resist expressing frustration that bubbles to the surface, but getting mad does not improve the situation. Anger is not perceived as love. Bluster is not a form of foreplay. Dumping guilt and fear onto a partner does not stimulate vaginal lubrication or penile hardness.

The biochemistry of the limbic system, which moderates survival instincts and sexual arousal, is influenced by good and bad life experiences. Add up enough bad experiences—when a lover feels dissed or endangered—and sexual attraction dissipates. It just un-happens.

Actually, it is possible to become aroused on command, but that is the topic of another book.

A common view is that falling out of love, and sexual attraction, is natural, will always be the case, and is a good argument for serial monogamy or non-monogamy. That argument may or may not be provable, but what I have seen in my personal life, and in session, is that revulsion can shift back to attraction within seconds. My perspective is that sexual attraction is more durable than most people realize. All that might be needed is to reverse the ego wounding.

Chapter 3 describes communication habits—normal, after-peak behavior—that subtly wound the ego, and can trigger a feeling of being attacked. That is the recommended "don't do" chapter. However, something disturbing will inevitably come up, so Chapter 4 addresses how to ease a threatened limbic system, instead of further agitating it.

The Path to Peace

The good news is that all relationships can dramatically improve. If I, a shy introvert, can become a relationship expert, so can you. The bad news is that you will have to do some things differently. More good news is that the changes I detail feel awesome, empowering, possibly magical, and even save time and energy.

I have loved sexual sensation ever since I discovered it, but it wasn't until my late thirties that I was introduced to the communication and emotional openness skills needed for sustainable sexual quality with another human. In my case, a human female.

I wasn't born an alpha male. I never had the desire to be the best, get rich, or command attention. To compete for desirable women at all, I had to find another way. Basically, the opposite way.

Instead of pumping myself up, I committed myself to discovering what it was about me that led to frustrating situations with current or prospective lovers, that caused my brain to freeze. Times when I felt sexually impotent and pathetic. And what was it about me that caused my lovers to feel that way too? I wanted to know, because I was very, very attached to having sex!

I discovered that it is super easy to block, turn off, or shut down a lover's natural attraction. This book fleshes out that key discovery, so you can nurture an attraction that lasts beyond the rush of first sex.

Perhaps out of a need for self-preservation, we tend to reject our partners when things get dicey—which makes things worse sexually and emotionally—instead of better. From my perspective, shame, insecurity, and fear related to sexual issues, consciously or not, underlie this downward relationship spiral. Unresolved hurts and unfulfilled needs that were once buried rise closer to the surface. Such revelations can shock a nervous system that has gotten dependent on the status quo.

Unplanned revelations can leak out during ordinary conversations about money or dishes and inflict unexpected damage. Combining statistics on married and unmarried couples, the average sexual relationship lasts only three years. Beyond that, one partner, or both, can't take the daily wear and tear.

The concepts and techniques in this book are designed to reduce that wear and tear to practically nothing, so both partners can respond to the slightest sexual stimulus that sparks between them.

Two of my clients are a highly successful married couple who have lots of sex, in spite of their delight in needling each other with sarcasm and criticisms. On occasion, however, real conflict breaks out. The urge to fight overcomes their good humor, and they contemplate breaking up.

After a few days of relationship hell, they get back to equilibrium. When I hear about the fights, it is hard for me not to laugh. When their blood pressures rise, communication dissolves into misunderstandings that are comically absurd.

This couple is better off than most who I see. At least they return to good sex after a fight. Many couples never recover. In my observation, there is a "tipping point" during interactions between partners, when an unexpected emotional buildup overtakes ordinary discussion or playful jousting. An unresolved hurt or unfilled need suddenly rises to the surface, turning friends into foes. Like a playful or languorous cat that inexplicably bites your fingers.

Conflict with our sexual partners can happen just as quickly and feel scarier than a little cat. More like a charging lion. Why does this happen? My theory is because sexual frustration wreaks such havoc with our egos. Sexual confidence, even reproductive fitness, may be at stake. If the subliminal fear is that sex with our partner has ended, that is a genuine existential threat.

The genuineness of a threat is in the eye of the beholder. Tension arises when one partner minimizes or ridicules our irrational fears. That is when the cat, or lion, or bear, bares its teeth and claws. That's when a lover takes anything, like a comment on a dirty shirt, seriously. Serious enough to verbally slash or bite.

Impulsive attacks or defenses happen before consideration of the harmful consequences. But there is a better way. Armed with knowledge and practice, the ego can become more fluid. Less like a delicate snowflake and more like a pool of water. A fluid ego is more likely to rein in a communication style that is pushing the interaction toward an emotional tipping point.

Should you never fight? Not if that is achieved solely by suppressing emotions. But fighting is unnecessary if a couple has enough emotional intelligence. That means encouraging the expression of vulnerable emotions.

Vulnerable emotions, like sadness, are not threatening and can attract compassion or empathy. Angry criticisms are an external cover for underlying hurt. In that sense, they are unjustified.

Anger is justified over an agreement violation. The violator has to accept that. Shared anger at something not related to the couple can be cathartic for both. Righteous anger, in defense of family, community, or the downtrodden, is to be commended.

But I submit that righteous anger does not apply toward a lover, since ego is the only thing being defended. The merit of such a defense is highly suspect. If you are aware of this concept, you may be more able to handle a wounded-ego attack pointed in your direction.

I speak directly to you, the reader, and write about you because I believe I know something about you. First, I have experienced everything I talk about, in all its pain and glory. Second, I have worked with enough private clients to see repeated problems and solutions.

This book describes many fundamental relating issues, and how they can be solved. The concepts and tools provided help you manage yourself, and your lover, partner, or spouse, during typical relationship tipping points, so you can minimize time in relationship hell and maximize pleasure.

Getting back to sex and coziness is what we wish for. The intensity of a fight can sometimes fuel a burning-hot sexual interlude. That can be a relieving reset. But more commonly, new hurts are added, nullifying long-term ease. A slow buildup of sexual frustration negatively impacts the quality and frequency of sex, thereby reducing opportunities to relieve relationship tension. It's a vicious circle.

I see sexual frustration and tension stress exhibited by couples every day in their body language and tone of voice. Studies have shown that brief periods of dramatic/life-threatening stress, like the occasional forest fire, or raid by a neighboring tribe, are actually healthy for humans. It's what we're designed for. But long-term, low-grade stress has the opposite effect. Chronic stress "may damage directly or through functional circuits practically all organs and tissues," according to the National Institutes of Health, eventually shortening lifespan.

General life stress, from work or child-rearing, is a constant that may not be completely fixable. However, dissolving sexual frustration can relieve one source of chronic stress, and offer a salve for others. That is one blessing of couple-hood.

Except for a short period during the falling-in-love phase, you will face aggravation, conflict, disagreement, upset, anger, discord, discomfort, and disappointment in relation to your lover. Most of the time these uncomfortable states are perplexing. You wonder why they happen, wish they wouldn't, and feel defeated by them when they pop up. Accumulated defeats can wear you down.

This book gives you the answers and tools you need to turn your home life into a fortress of life-giving support instead of a pit of crippling anxiety. A happy and fulfilled life is natural and close at hand. It costs nothing and even takes less energy than the typical struggle.

Practice is essential, however, because when you feel attacked, you need to have a moderating response, such as deep breathing, wired into your limbic system. A response that slows the action down enough to generate more accurate thinking.

No one gets the luxury of a warning. Your lover will not say "Timeout. OK. I've decided that now is a good time to dump on you. It will feel really good to me! Ready?"

Practice trains reactions, like martial arts, so you can productively respond to tanking or threats while the neocortex—the rational part of your brain—is temporarily offline. The neocortex needs time to bring in a more complete understanding of causes and effects, so a sudden increase in tension does not escalate into a limbic-limbic battle. So you don't automatically reach for your sword.

2

The Anatomy of Discord

Humans of all genders and orientations are drawn to each other for sex. They are rewarded with an increase in dopamine. Under the influence of a dopamine high, lovers can do no wrong.

Therapeutic-grade MDMA, street name Ecstasy, has the same effect, which is why it was used legally for couples therapy by thousands of psychotherapists in the US from 1980 to 85.

Illegality now makes Ecstasy quality highly suspect. Pure MDMA has two powerful effects that can help us see how naturally occurring dopamine impacts relationships. One, MDMA dramatically increases empathy. Two, it boosts self-confidence to the point where the ego is not threatened by almost anything a partner says or does.

Female Lover: "I would love to try a threesome with two men."

Male Lover: "Wow! You are so cool."

They kiss and snuggle for a few minutes.

Male Lover: "I am so turned on by Keira Knightley. She has my perfect female body type."

Female Lover: "Totally! She is unbelievably beautiful."

Both partners responded to potentially challenging statements with 100 percent support.

The dopamine reward for sex and love is so compelling mere mortals cannot resist. But what then? After a certain length of time, dopamine production decreases. The feeling of being in love wears off.

Why does nature do this to us? My theory: So our longer term judgment returns. A high that never ends leads to poor survival decisions, like not gathering enough food for winter.

Our minds return to normal, and we view our lovers and partners more critically. And crucially important, our egos regain their fragility. The power of dopamine to give us supreme self-confidence goes away. Our typical fears and insecurities rise again to the fore. And no one activates them more efficiently than our intimate partners.

When our fears and insecurities come back, the contrast to the initial phase of romance is soul-crushing. The dopamine-rush phase and subsequent crash phase are emphasized through evolution. Nature's priority is reproduction. It doesn't care about other consequences, like anxiety.

Female Lover: "I'm hungry."

Male Lover: "You can't be hungry. We just ate an hour ago!"

A year earlier he would have said with a smile, "Cool, I just happen to have an apple and some peanut butter in my CamelBak. Wouldn't it be nice to snuggle by the creek and watch the water?" That would have been dopamine-high speak. Now he's irritated by his partner. Little criticisms and judgments have built up over the year. They leak out.

Female Lover: "Dickhead!" She is hurt by his irritation and strikes back. A period of silence ensues while their bodies stew in stress hormones.

As the crash period takes hold, lovers express sides of themselves not focused on each other. Career goals, exercise needs, political or spiritual beliefs, the pull of friends and family, and even attractions to other potential sexual partners reassert themselves.

Tender egos become pitiful. Barely perceptible thoughts form, like "You mean I am not the most important thing to you every minute of every day?" or "What, you're not happy with me exactly as I am?" or "You don't really like my limitations?"

Our lovers don't give us the answers we want to hear, and it freaks us out. If we allowed ourselves to react as we honestly felt, we would collapse into a puddle and cry. Instead, we conclude that we have to prop up our egos. This pattern of ego defense is automatic and often takes the form of lashing out. Attacking. The attacks and defenses can be subtle and confusing. We don't understand what we are doing.

The Delicate Ego

What makes us behave this way? Pain. Evolution has coded us to avoid pain. It's instinctive, like instantly pulling your hand away from a hot flame. A challenge to ego elicits painful, disorienting, or dissociative sensations.

The ego signals its displeasure, hoping to stop the perceived challenge. Immediately. It urges us to kill the challenging message or messenger (our lover). Since ego thinks everything was hunky-dory before, it blames the messenger for the disruption.

The word *ego* means "I" in Latin. The experience of "I" is an approximation of the self or identity. It feels like a whole thing rather than a collection of nodes in the brain. The illusion of wholeness is the "I," or ego. This shorthand version of our operating system enables a quick response to threats.

If we see a man wielding a combat knife headed our direction, our bodies flood with chemicals that urge us to take action. The "I" experiences this as fear. Fear is an emotion. It is not rational.

A lover can become the source of irrational fear by implying a status demotion. Earlier in the relationship, they would not have mentioned garlic farts. Now that the subject comes up, the ego's feeling about its importance takes a hit. Self-confidence, hence the ego, is challenged.

Of course, our sense of status, our belief in how important we are to our lover, is invented by our minds. Our actual status is higher or lower than we realize. Lovers seldom discuss, moment by moment, their status with each other. The result is less information, but also less potential for negative interpretations, so a reasonable trade-off.

If one partner leaves the relationship, that is a clear status indicator. But there are thousands of lesser signals, such as a look of disappointment, which ego is vulnerable to. Such vulnerabilities can rock, or wreck, our worlds.

Elevations and demotions of status flutter through our minds all the time and affect our moods and behavior. Most people don't track these fluctuations, so are surprised by mismatches. When one lover notices that the other lover's shirt is dirty, a status or self-image bubble is burst.

Uncharitably, one could say this behavior is infantile. It is perhaps a vestige of inconsistent parental approval, leaving us sensitive to lack of approval. As adults, the only threat is a status demotion, but the same sensitivity gets triggered.

Reactions to fear can be uncontrollable. Fear of loss can be so intense that partners may stay in abusive relationships. On a milder level, fear of losing the cuddly feeling may be the primary motivator.

The ego reacts to real and imagined threats similarly, through a change in body chemistry that gets our attention. The ego is quick to exercise its authority, since it represents our identities built up over decades.

Our bodies feel disoriented when a lover who used to delight in every detail of us sings a different tune. It's like we are HAL in the movie *2001: A Space Odyssey* and our programming bars are being pulled out. We fight to keep the only things we know, as unexpected sensations escalate.

For me, ego challenge disorientation is like acid reflux, causing light-headedness, even if there is no pain. I become achingly self-conscious, and feel like a caricature of myself, awkwardly bumbling around like a puppet without strings.

Other common symptoms are sweaty palms, shallow breath, and an inability to maintain eye contact. The limbic system is only a portion of the ego's neural circuitry, but the body symptoms it can produce are dominating.

Learning how ego-challenging experiences, like rejection, affect us requires an increased awareness of body sensations and postures. The body doesn't lie. Somewhere the body is experiencing sensations when rejection is happening. The sooner one notices the symptoms, the sooner one can implement a remediation technique.

The Need for Skills

You may spend most of the time laughing, making love, eating, or hiking with your lover. That is great! But too often the emotional pain of an ego challenge is unbearable, and a fight ensues. Feeling wretched, bruised, and beaten, you wonder if the pain is worth it.

Fights are disproportionately significant compared to their time span, perhaps only one percent of a couple's waking hours together. But harmful words and actions are not forgotten. They are archived in mind and body memory. From there, they affect future thoughts and feelings.

When you blow up at someone, it takes time to get back to a good feeling. It's easier, takes far less time, and is less costly to use emotional intelligence instead. The difference can be fifteen minutes of discomfort before closer connection, versus five days of wretchedness that then seems to wane, but not entirely.

When the dopamine high wears off, couples need interpersonal skills to mediate the tension discomfort. If they don't, then destructive communications will proliferate. Observing couples in session, I see how quickly communication goes off track. Usually within thirty seconds. At home, such interactions never get back on track, leading to unprocessed resentments. Accumulation of these mildly painful moments reduces happiness and attraction to each other.

Off-Track communication sample:

Blair: "How do you feel about me modeling for an art class?"

Drew: "We don't need the money."

Blair: "I wouldn't be primarily doing it for the money."

Drew: "Why then?"

Blair: "Just for fun."

Drew: "You call that a reason?"

In this example, a simple question has turned into an inquisition within the first two sentences. The interaction starts with "How do you feel...." Did Drew reply to this question? No. The first reply was an analytical statement. The second reply was a question, and the third was a criticism. In less than thirty seconds, this couple is feeling uncomfortable.

What would be an On-Track interaction?

Blair: "How do you feel about me modeling for an art class?"

Drew: Pause for thought. "I feel some irritation."

Blair: "Uh Huh. Can you say more about that?"

Drew: "Yes. The irritation is rising up in relation to an uncontrollable fear."

Blair: "What is the fear?"

Drew: "I'm afraid of that moment when I visualize a bunch of people gawking at my nude wife."

Blair: Moves in for a hug. "Oh honey, that's so adorable."

The lovers smile while they hug. A good vibe is set for further discussion.

Most couples do not have the required communication skills to correct an interaction that goes off track. Or connection habits to touch base, clear the air, and bring each other up to date. Connecting is an art that combines skills I discuss throughout this book. Despite recurring relationship pain, most people do not seek out the means to make things better. Or they reject the notion that there is a problem.

But ignoring or denying problems is not a successful strategy since the real self can't be hidden. It reveals itself in tone of voice, word choice, body language, and behaviors. Discomfort and anxiety inevitably rise. Eventually, something has to blow.

Blowing Up

Reactions are fast in attack-and-defend mode, like jumping off the trail from the sound of a rattlesnake rattle. But it's confusing. Part of you is terrified, and part of you wonders why. However, your body feels that you *are* afraid. It remembers disapproving, rejecting, or even abusive moments from your past. Fight-or-flight is activated.

Due to the circumstances of our personal histories, we have developed instinctive responses to words and situations with our sexual partners. We try not to flinch, since that would be a signal of weakness, but our partners see us react anyway. If a high-speed video camera recorded us, we would be amused, or horrified, by what we would see ourselves doing.

Eyes widen, brows furrow. We rock back and start to raise our arms to defend ourselves. We recoil from words. The subconscious notices the recoil, and initiates thoughts in sync with a defensive posture, such as "I have to get out of here!" The body feels threatened, and the mind matches it.

You don't like what is happening. You observe yourself acting weird. Repressed anger and resentment bubble up. In the heat of the moment, you act uncivilized. Your dark side takes over, and you blame your lover for provoking it.

The dissociative state of ego challenge reduces intelligent functionality, leading to insecure, and paranoid, conclusions. The mind in this state doesn't search for verifying or correcting data. One might believe perfect mental clarity is operating, but in reality, it is the primal, emotional self. The primal self, or id in Freud's terms, feels justified to act on its impulses. The rational mind is a dead nothing in comparison.

A smoothly functioning mind is useful, but ironically, ultimate functionality is only achieved through increased facility with primitive emotions.

Polarization

As blood pressure rises, and primitive emotions emerge, partners default to well-worn patterns or positions. If one partner tends to be rational, then their rationality will increase. In response, an emotional partner will become more emotional.

Partners polarize around a wide range of axes, such as more sex versus less sex, or tight versus free spending. Polarization happens regardless of gender or orientation, and increases the anguish of any tense situation.

A particularly common polarization for heterosexual couples is along gender lines. Women are usually more capable of sharing their feelings than men. But men are often irritated in response to emotional expression or nonlinear conversation. This dynamic weakens sexual receptiveness.

Men have the abilities they need to be good partners, but the dominant culture emphasizes technical over emotional skills. The result is a male ego that is threatened by emotions since that is not its area of expertise.

But that expertise is precisely what is needed for satisfying intimate relationships. Men fall into helplessness when challenged by their women. Their feeling of sexual potency evaporates. A man fears any hint that his woman is withdrawing her sexual willingness.

She wants him to melt her, but he gets stuck in feelings of incompetence. Her nature includes a little testing of him. Commitment to him is not a blank check. She wants him to be reliably loving. This testing behavior is not under her conscious control, so not a justification for blame from a man.

When a woman is sad, testing, or even exuberantly happy, if her man can't meet her mood, he will try to extinguish it. This squash response disturbs the female limbic system, leaving her feeling emotionally and sexually unsafe. Every day, and long-term, women want to feel loved. The universe of actions that demonstrate love is endless, but an action of some type is required. Unfortunately, as the man's dopamine wears off, he is less capable of generating the creativity, emotional openness, and sexual interest that could motivate an act of love. It's a downward spiral.

When the dopamine high wears off, the vulnerable underbelly of each lover is exposed and susceptible to wounding. Rational analysis can't prevent the wounding. Data will be lacking, along with respectful and creative responses.

It's necessary to learn new responses, so you can do *something* useful when you face an ego challenge. You can learn to stay calm, have a relaxed face, inquisitive eyes, and deeper breath to counter a defensive posture. A relaxed demeanor disarms your opponent (who in this case is also your partner).

It's all about how fast you can drop into a supportive instead of a resistive state of being. The quicker you do it, the less grief you will suffer, since an attack, or counterattack, has the opposite effect from protecting the ego. It provokes further ego challenge. Back and forth until both partners are crushed.

The crash phase does not *have* to lead to a breakup. If you can minimize blowups and maximize reconnections, the being-in-love period will be significantly extended, and long-term oxytocin/vasopressin tenderness achieved, punctuated by frequent periods of dopamine-fueled hot sex. Hot sex is evidence that something is going right. Discord may then dissipate by itself, like the morning mist on a placid lake.

3

Poking the Bear

Bears are the alpha predators in their natural habitats and are agitated by humans entering their territory. A small mistake, made by not understanding bear behavior, can result in an attack, which is high on the list of life's scary moments.

Powerful paws and deadly jaws are avoided by not crossing a line in the bear's psyche that triggers its territorial or self-defense mechanisms. By not "poking" the bear. If your lover snaps at you, or gives you the cold shoulder, it is likely you have activated a bearlike defense. As a "human naturalist," you can learn from such reactions. You can seek to better understand your partner's bear language.

The natural role of your lover is as your most enthusiastic and committed supporter. A foundation from which you can grow and excel in the world. If, however, this primary relationship is a struggle, a considerable amount of life energy is drained away, leaving fewer resources for happiness and productivity.

This chapter describes some typical habits that wreak havoc with your biggest supporter and lead to bearish agitation. These habits might seem small and petty when you look at the list. But they are not. If your lover has to devote time and effort to withstanding them, resistance to you hardens. Then one day they can longer have sex with you.

As the in-love phase wears off, our less enlightened selves reemerge. Impatience, frustration, and jumping to conclusions become more frequent. We're not as happy, and we get cranky. We express less caring. Frustrations come out unedited.

We act as though our lovers should be impervious to our inflictions. That we should be able to vent without consequences. Unfortunately, there are consequences.

What most people don't realize is that all of us are more insecure than we appear. We put on a strong front. But the facade has cracks. Painful words make it through as easily as water through a sieve. The tricky part is that you might not even know what those words are. You can see a little hurt on a partner's face and be annoyed by their sensitivity.

"What the hell is wrong with you?" you might think. "Can't you handle yourself?"

Yes, that would be ideal. But few of us are trained for the exposure of intimacy. Your supporter takes a confidence hit when you are petulant. Since sexiness is rooted in confidence, sexiness takes a hit too.

We notice how poorly received our cranky impulses are, but don't know why, and can't stop ourselves anyway. Learning to recognize the symptoms that precede a destructive impulse gives us a choice to quash it before it comes out.

Am I advocating suppression? Yes. I understand how strong the urge is to say or do something that will hurt. Just Don't Do It. Self-control will serve you well. If in doubt, wait.

Waiting helps you notice the emotions you are feeling. If you are a sexual being, you cannot escape the world of emotions. Believe it or not, that is a good thing. Life would be too easy otherwise. You would have less motivation to grow and live to your potential.

The impulse to attack or defend comes from emotions buried underneath the surface. Pausing before acting gives you time to access those emotions, acknowledge them, and take responsibility for them. To take command of your mood ship.

You will often be in a mood mismatch with your partner. One of you will be more up or down. Either way can be unnerving. Not knowing what to do leads to mistakes and unexpected reactions (blowups) from a partner.

Blowups always have a buildup. Couples can reduce blowup frequency with communication that reduces the number of emotional tipping points.

Emotions come and go. That is their purpose. They are a way to feel fully alive, recenter, or clear the air. Ego defense interferes with this process. Attempting to quash or derail emotions makes them grow larger.

You are *already* in a fight if you resist or try to stop your partner from expressing their emotions, or their authentic selves, if that expression is truly about just them, and not a judgment of you.

Emotions are not like a bleeding wound, which is helped by applying direct pressure. Emotions are like a forest that intermittently needs to burn for optimum health.

"I thought you just said to suppress emotions." Glad you noticed! What should be suppressed is the urge to inflict damage on your partner. That would be an externalization of your issues. Vulnerable emotions do not attack.

Emotions need to be expressed, but there is a time and place. A recipient for all of your emotions is a required resource. That could be a friend or therapist. Your lover will probably be there for vulnerable emotions, like sadness. Don't expect that for anger.

If frustration tips toward anger, momentum can be hard to pull back. No matter how ridiculous it might seem in retrospect, there is a tendency to keep going once we start in that direction. Backing down, or reversing directions in the face of feedback, might be viewed as weakness. Thus, the original position hardens.

Heterosexual men are particularly susceptible to this dynamic. "A hard man is good to find" refers to a fit body, and powerful erection, not emotional rigidity. Women can be just as rigid as men, but may use more nuanced arguments.

Since you are reading this book, you're the one who can change inflammatory habits. The time and effort involved is worth it. As in a financial investment, it is ten times as hard to earn back a loss (make it up to your partner) as it is to not lose it (harm your partner) in the first place.

In my sessions with couples, we almost always uncover a defining moment, or set of moments, that led to a severe distancing from each other. Those moments are often brief, in the range of five to fifteen seconds. As little as the misunderstanding of a single word has made the difference between a marriage dissolving and getting back to tender love and playful sex.

It can take an enormous amount of time and effort to go back and reconstruct the moment to the point where both partners agree on what happened. My rule-of-thumb ratio is one hour of reconstruction/deconstruction for every minute of hurtful outburst, severe misunderstanding, or complete communication breakdown. Yes, that is a sixty-to-one ratio.

Does that give you some motivation to do things differently in the first place?

Below is a list of automatic responses you may have to your happy, sad, fearful, or angry partner, which add fuel to a smoldering emotional fire. Try to take in that you do these things, often without knowing it. That is not your fault. You were not trained for the reality of relationships.

After reading the list of habits, and the explanations, you may still respond habitually. That's OK. It's never too late to try again. And to give lovers another chance when they are being merciless. Try to give as much slack as possible.

The habit corrections of this chapter will dramatically reduce the number of conflicts that escalate into real fights. You will be amazed how grateful your lover will be if you eliminate just *one* habit.

Bear-Poking Habits

- Ignoring Your Lover
- Taking Things Personally
- Defending Yourself
- Attacking Back (Verbally)
- Making Assumptions
- Rehearsing a Response
- Blocking or Sidetracking with Content
- Invalidating
- Criticizing or Judging
- Giving Advice or an Opinion
- Insisting on Being Right
- Analyzing or Interpreting
- Placating or Patronizing
- Interrupting an Emotional Expression

Ignoring Your Lover

It's useful to keep in mind that lovers have an insecure side. They want to matter. If you are obsessively focused on your own activities and thoughts, you may miss your lover's "bids," or attempts at connection. Research conducted by psychologist Dr. John Gottman, at the Gottman Institute, predicts the viability of relationships within 94 percent accuracy, based on responses to bids alone.

A bid could be anything, from a gentle massaging of shoulders to an inconsequential statement.

Wife: "I see a Western kingbird out in the mulberry tree."
Husband: "Harrumph!"

Maybe you hate birds or interruptions, but there is a large qualitative difference between "harrumph!" and "nice," or "awesome." The grunt communicates displeasure of some type. Alas, your lover will be boring, will repeat things, and be excited about things you are not excited about. That is just the way it is.

Over time, little rejections add up, however. It doesn't take much effort to give a little acknowledgment. Your acknowledgment helps keep your lover's confidence up, which you want. The more a lover's confidence dips, the more need for reassurance, which could become a burden.

A partner's bid for attention can pop up at any moment. I was feeling a coffee rush one morning and absorbed in writing a scene when my partner Cheryl danced into my office space. She was pumped after a coaching session with one of her favorite clients.

I turned to face her, smiled broadly, and undulated with her as she sang the last lines of "All That Jazz." We embraced, with a little playful fondling, then she moved on to her next task of the day, beaming.

The entire interaction took only two minutes. Cheryl had interrupted me, but I didn't chastise her. Instead, I shifted into welcoming her joy. She lustfully absorbed my attention and was quickly satisfied. I felt an echo boost, from joining in with her jubilance, that enhanced the rest of my writing session.

I know, from less happy relationship times, the price I paid when I militantly refused to pop out of my personal bubble. It appeared as though I had protected my work, project, or study time, but many minutes, and even hours were lost struggling to regain equanimity. I was too stirred up. Too angry.

Later, there was a hill to climb getting back into comfort with my partner. That took time and effort. Tired of repeatedly falling into a hole, I changed tactics and discovered a magical formula: The more swiftly and impressively you acknowledge your lover, the less time and energy it takes.

Every moment with your lover can go in an up or down direction. You literally hold your lover's heart in your hands. Ironically, the more consistently attention needs are met, the more fulfilled a partner feels, which naturally reduces attention needs.

Your lover will blossom from your habit of watering all bids. From you noticing and responding to what's on your lover's surface. Under the surface is trickier. If something is up with your lover, you can discount or ignore it. Perhaps you are mistaken, or it's just something your lover needs to handle on their own.

But if it persists, it's best to be preemptive. Whatever is going on is already affecting both of you. Unexpressed thoughts and feelings have a way of leaking out, often at conflict-inducing moments.

Apprehension may keep you from trying to find out what

is up with your partner. You may fear poking the bear. Your lover's emotional animal could threateningly rise on its back legs. Or it could pretend to be dead. The situation might feel over your head. Try not to let fear stop you, since partners may interpret fear as rejection.

Catastrophizing thoughts about potential conflict are almost always worse than the actual moment of discussion or inquiry. When you proceed with open-mindedness, useful information is exchanged.

Tap into your natural communication abilities. With your help, your lover will feel relief by getting something off their chest. Successful transitions from anxiety and fear to completed negotiations feel good and motivate doing it again.

If it looks like a time to engage, there is always a way. What you can notice about each other is an indicator of your abilities. Showing abilities gives you cred and will demonstrate that you care.

Caring is a better habit than ignoring. The "act" of caring can stimulate genuine caring within the actor, so give it a shot. Seeing, observing, and receiving caring is infinitely better than rejection. It is a ground-level affirmation of connection. Err on the side of more engagement. You don't have to be at your best. Just jump in. Interacting can make you feel better if you are not running a negative, or resistant dialogue in your head. I know the healing benefit of engagement is possible, even for introverts like myself.

Whatever is going on between the two of you, there is an opportunity to learn about your reactions, and upgrade them, instead of perpetuating a cycle of annoyance. Here is a radical upgrade: Imagine that every moment of interaction with your lover contains the possibility of pleasure. The content of words, the eloquence of voice, or the gentlest touch, can be received sensually. How deeply can you receive every type of contact with your lover as a pleasurable sensation?

This is a practice of honoring oneself, one's partner, and life itself. The harder such a practice seems, the more relationship data there is for you to discover.

Taking Things Personally

You are taking something personally if you suddenly have a strong reaction. Otherwise, you would just be curious.

What if someone said:

"There is no God."

"We must preserve the sanctity of marriage."

"Men are rapists."

"Women are too needy."

"Mercury Retrograde is screwing up my cell phone."

You might be offended by one or more of these statements, which could raise your hackles. You might want to argue against the statement. Such reactions are examples of taking things personally. Your first response is a visceral or emotional one, instead of an intellectually curious one.

A lover's after-peak words or behaviors may seem strange or offensive to you. Less thoughtful. More sensitive. Less curious. More opinionated. Less tolerant. More religious, or atheistic. More self-centered. Such changes could come as a shock. Your tendency to take something personally has returned.

Imagine you are out on a dinner date, and your lover casually intones, "I noticed there's a sex-toy shop across the street. We could pop in after dinner."

A trickle of fear-induced adrenaline shoots through your body. "What's wrong with our sex life?" jumps into your mind. If you interpret your lover's words negatively, your mood is wrecked. Before you have time to think through possible meanings, your body reacts. You have attacked yourself.

Your lover presented browsing a sex-toy store with a delicious gleam in the eye, hoping to excite you. Instead, you have contracted within yourself. A glorious or significant moment turns into "Ugh." It's hard to get the glory back.

Instead of having to dig out of a hole, you can train yourself to believe that such bids are not about you. "This is not about me" can be your first response, like breathing. The slightest lag time gives you a chance to formulate a more life-giving interpretation of content.

An interpretation is an invention of your mind. It is not a fact. Discard unhelpful interpretations. Life is more peaceful if you stick with the facts.

The facts you have: A sex-toy shop is across the street. Your lover has proposed, with a smile, an after-dinner activity. What could be easier than embracing the idea? "That sounds great! I haven't been to one for years. I wonder what new products are available. This is so cool. I didn't know you were interested in toy stores."

Thus begins an intimate conversation. If you have fears to share, fine. Feelings add juice. Not succumbing to a deflating interpretation may lead to a night that changes your lives together.

I know how difficult it can be to manage your thoughts. I grew up the most insecure and self-conscious person I knew. To achieve reasonable functioning, I learned to divide myself into parallel tracks. One track was flowing, effortless connection with my lover. The other was isolated self-consciousness. I discovered I could choose the connection flow and discard the isolated one.

Being in sync with a beloved is one of the best feelings ever. But something may come up that stimulates your dislikes, fears, and insecurities. Specific topics will frighten or offend you. Such responses are correlated with cultural programming. You may resent that programming, so ask yourself: "Is this urge to react truly me, or is it just my programming?"

My journey has included jettisoning homophobia, for example. Through experimentation, and going beyond my preconceived notions, I came to understand where my physical-contact boundaries with men actually were.

You never know when you will uncontrollably take something personally.

Partner 1: "I hate my mother!"

Partner 2: "Don't say that!"

Partner 2's response overrode partner 1, making it about Partner 2's inability to handle an emotional expression. The emotional energy of "hate" may dangerously swing in Partner 2's direction.

Challenging situations arise, and we freak. There seems to be no escape. It's particularly painful when a partner brings up a weakness we have. Such a moment is so different from the being-in-love phase. An unwanted ego challenge is thrown in our face when the word "you" is in the sentence.

Woman: "I need you to last longer."

Man: "I noticed that you've gained weight."

Ouch! An insecurity you have no defense for is unmercifully exposed. Partner status could be at stake. This intensity of self-focus is like an invisible taser that shocks away the blissful feeling of connection.

Self-centeredness is the default in nature. A rutting buck

has no concern for the well-being of other males in the herd. If you walk toward a cat, it will move out of your way, even though you know with absolute certainty you will not step on it. The cat overreacts to protect itself.

This self-focus default has survival value. If ancestral humans overreacted to a sound in the grass, thinking it was a lion instead of just the wind, our species was more likely to survive.

We have now survived and proliferated better than any other species, but we still overreact (take things personally), before we even realize it. Our five senses take in the environment around us and filter first for anything that might threaten us.

This response is ideal if you are "on point" with your squad in a war zone. But in more typical human interactions, self-focus separates you from people. If you are always wondering how everything will affect *you*, you hijack the energy.

You might just be in a bad mood. That's OK. Sharing your state is communication fuel. But always letting your fears, insecurities, anxieties, and limitations block your full engagement sends a message that others will feel. That message is interpreted as rejection even if you say nothing. Your face reveals your state.

Being unaware of this habit is possible. Erring on the side of your limits may feel like normal behavior to you. But that tendency is socially deflating. It lowers interest in you. What is the real you? It is not only the thoughts running through your head. The real you includes the times you are in flow, are pumped up, having a great time, and acting spontaneously.

No matter how painful or offensive something is to your ego, taking it personally makes the personal growth that would fix weaknesses, or ease self-defeating attitude towards them, harder to achieve.

What can you do when you are sinking? Try not to interpret what you see or hear as an attack. Share what is happening to you vulnerably. "I am so afraid of not being perfect for you," for example. The purpose is to hear yourself speaking the fear. It is a step toward releasing it, instead of amplifying it in your head. This quality of sharing invites empathy from your partner.

Listening to your lover's perspective on you can be scary. You may believe speaking your vulnerabilities puts the relationship at risk. But your lover knows about them already. The vulnerable truth is running you no matter how hard you hide it. The effort to hide is a tell.

Your lover has sympathy for your struggles. Your lover is with you until they walk out the door and don't come back. So ease your burden by revealing yourself. No relationship is worth never growing and changing. There is an element of risk. If your lover is irretrievably offended by you, then the relationship was not sustainable anyway. Better to find out sooner rather than later.

Your lover makes everything more real by putting pressure on what you hide. Lovers want to know what you are hiding and won't offer support if you defend your weaknesses. The only path of relief is diving into the cauldron of personal growth.

Your reactions to disturbing stimuli tell you when it's time to dive. Unless random violence or a freak of nature comes at you, the outside world is not the cause of your most disturbing reactions. Those reactions are within you, and therefore your responsibility.

The degree to which you take things personally is the degree to which you limit yourself. Lovers can have compassion for your issues, but they hate being controlled by those issues. Our lovers wants to live their best life, and for you to as well. They do not want you to limit them, or be attacked by the defense of your self-defeating habits.

If your lover challenges your need for control or your understanding of reality, that is your problem. Adverse reactions to your lover are your stuff. If your stuff is causing a problem, then you have to work on it. The more you work on your stuff, the more you can stay engaged and connected with your lover.

Disturbing reactions to your lover are a rich source of information. Do you honestly like your lover? No one is perfect, but it is important to like a sizable subset of your lover's traits. For relationship longevity, you can train yourself to notice and enhance your positive reactions, like the tingle of sexual arousal from seeing their naked body.

If you strategically edit negative interpretations, you avoid unconsciously smacking your partner down and being perpetually oppositional. It may feel that a counter/oppositional impulse is the "true" you, so why should you block it? The problem is, those impulses could just be programs from your past.

No matter how dysfunctional or admirable our families, schools, churches, and friends were growing up, we absorbed a huge chunk of that conditioning. Under pressure, we parrot it out as our part of our core "self."

I propose that running legacy programming rarely *feels* like the true you. More like you are watching yourself act a part in a movie, and you don't like the role. The real you is nuanced and takes time to discover. Through trial and error. When you try new things, and let in the experience, your knowledge of your likes and dislikes expands.

Every day, something happens that challenges your current assessment of yourself. That is where the action of life is if you can embrace it.

The real you is not rigid. A softer habit of reacting with awe and interest makes it safer for lovers to share their truths. Truth leads deeper into intimacy. That can be scary since the outcome is unpredictable. Unpredictably uncomfortable, and unpredictably fabulous. The fabulous path opens up possibilities that are unimaginable any other way. Much like being in love.

You can insist on staying within the confines of limitations, comforts, beliefs, and knowns you think you need, and reject everything else, but that insistence will push your lover away.

You have to up your game. The less you take things personally, the more you can handle any situation that comes your way. Even if the word "you" is in the sentence, it is not about you. I know how hard it is to not feel judged or criticized at that moment.

But, *everything* a partner says is more a reflection of them than you. Why is the topic coming up now? What emotion is being expressed? What content is that emotion based on? Even when "you" are in the sentence, if you don't take that personally, you can be present to hear all that a lover has to say.

Defending Yourself

Alexis: "You never take out the garbage!"
Jules: "Yes I do!"

Isn't it automatic to respond that way? A blustery defense is laid down before the evidence is fully considered.

A sneaky defense is a technically accurate interpretation of language that misses the actual meaning. In the above example, Jules focused on the word "never," since she could remember taking the garbage out once in the last three months. So Alexis was incorrect. But not by much.

The actual meaning of the garbage accusation: "I take out the garbage so often, it looks to me like you never do. That makes me feel disrespected."

The point of the statement is a feeling, not an investigative report. Memories from three months ago can be inaccurate. But a feeling is current. One can be compassionate toward a feeling. Compassion, or empathy, helps a partner feel heard. That might be all they need.

In reality, there is no defense against feelings. They just exist. One of you is feeling disrespected. An argument about the exact degree of any garbage hauling discrepancy does not assuage the feeling of disrespect. Feelings are a bid for support. Defensiveness trashes that bid. You can't go back in time and redo an imbalance, if there is one, but you can switch into effusive appreciation.

Jules: "Hmmm. I haven't been tracking it, but I am *grateful* you are so responsible for the garbage. Thank you for all that effort."

Gratitude is welcome. A twinge of tension could become a kissy moment. The immediate de-escalation of tension can then lead to more vulnerability on both sides, which makes a successful negotiation to handle the imbalance possible.

The defensive approach leads to an argument over who has the most accurate memory of garbage hauling over the last three months. Both partners lose. Memory is not accurate. We bias our memory to support our beliefs about ourselves.

I recommend jettisoning arguments based on memory. You either have provable facts or not. Even if you have documents, the point is a lover's perception, not the exact details.

One of the useful purposes of a partner is to challenge

the accuracy of our self-concepts. But if our partner holds a different view of us, it can feel like an attack. We hate it if doubt is expressed about our competency, moral character, actions, or statements.

A lover's doubt is disconcerting. It is hard not to put up a defense. But defending yourself is like saying your partner is a liar.

Alexis: "Your breath smells like garlic."

Jules: "But I didn't eat any garlic!"

This is a jumping-to-conclusions defense. A partner made a statement. The statement does not indicate that there is a problem. Is garlic breath bad or good? Does the partner care? Does it make the partner hungry for pizza? One doesn't know what the statement means.

A defensive reaction means the statement was taken as a criticism or accusation. Nobody likes to be falsely accused. It is useful to wait for the actual meaning of statements to be clear before replying. Take the time to let the message in before responding, so your mind can reduce all the words to their clearest content.

It takes concentration to focus on the meaning of words if an accusation or criticism comes your way, but such focus is super-useful for steering communication toward understanding and progress, instead of a fight.

Concentration helps your mind filter out automatic defenses and click into categorization. What type of communication is this? What is the exact topic? Are the words rational, or emotional? Is there a request here, or not?

Only a small percentage of a lover's communications are an analysis of you. It is your sensitivities and habits that push you to defend, after inventing criticisms that your lover was not thinking.

If the word "you" in a critical sentence is directed at

you, take it with a grain of salt. It's possible that your lover is cranky, stressed, or in some other way compromised. Try to take that into account, and first give empathy to their stressed state.

All social animals are subject to the debilitating effects of stress, but as high as 80 percent of primates suffer from it, as documented from wild baboon studies in *Behave: The Biology of Humans at Our Best and Worst* by Robert Sapolsky. The more compromised we are by stress, the more likely it is that we will act from attack-and-defend mode.

A hurtful lashing out is simply a reflection of pain. Start out with the least-threatening categorization. Next, take in the content. If you are being honest, does your lover have a valid point, discounting any negative shading? Our lovers want us to be our best. If we let that in, we can improve.

Partner input is often useful. Celebrate it. It's useful, cathartic, or entertaining. If you are hurt by your partner instead of entertained, feel the pain. Why is it there? What emotion underlies the pain you are experiencing? Guilt or shame is often involved.

Guilt evolved to motivate us to align with cultural norms. But most of us have been over-guilted. Guilt is appropriate if you have broken an agreement, or been pointlessly hurtful. Use that guilt to offer a makeup.

Shame is a biggie. Our lovers easily highlight our sexual inadequacies, insecurities, fears, taboos, limitations, kinks, and quirks. Since sexual shame is usually the strongest shame we have, reducing that shame is a foundation of your ability to not be defensive. If shame is not activated, you have nothing to defend. You just enjoy being you. Provided your sexual behavior is not harmful, if your lover is upset by it then it is their issue. Reducing sexual shame also opens the way to less shame about all other aspects of ourselves.

Imagine that you like to bite when you get aroused. If you are good at it, your lover will probably like it. If not, they may ask you not to do it. However, if your lover says, "You're sick," when you bite, that would be shaming. If you've worked on your shame, the judgment won't push you into defensive mode. You will understand that your lover is skin sensitive, inexperienced, brainwashed, or perhaps had a previous biting-negative experience. These responses can be viewed compassionately. You can bring your lover into the biting world, accept your lover as is, or break up. A lover's differences from you is a test of your sexual frustration management skills.

As a species, we are learning that sexual preferences are a core component of identity. That is reflected in changing laws that prioritize sexual freedom over religious injunctions.

The more you work on your shame, the more deeply you can dive into the real you, unburdened by your cultural programming. The clearer you are about your innate strengths, weaknesses, morals, and values, the less your partner will stimulate your shame response.

I will make a blanket statement: You never have to feel like a "bad" person. For sure, you will get cranky, and say or do harmful things. That is bad behavior. Accept it, and own it. But it is not a reflection of your whole being. It is just a slip-up. Make up for it and improve your behavior.

A non-defensive attitude relaxes tension over one lover making more money, being more attractive, being more sexually adventurous, or seeming to have more fun. An attitude of not defending reduces the potential seriousness of a conflict. It gives your lover a chance to blow off steam. Not defending defuses situations. Defending escalates them.

A defensive response means you have taken something

personally. Otherwise, you would simply be discussing a topic. It's hard not to take an accusation personally if it is inaccurate. But such an accusation could be viewed humorously.

"Why did you jump out the window?" Since you didn't, the accusation is absurd. Laughing is a way of saying so.

"You idiot!" Ouch. Not so easy to laugh about. This insult is an emotional outburst. It has a cathartic value for the emoting partner, but is harmful to the receiver, unless it is ignored. You know you are not an idiot, so you don't have to take it seriously. Your partner has just slipped into attack mode.

"Can you restate that in a way that expresses what you are unhappy about, instead of attacking me?" Hopefully, an apology will come with it.

Displeasure should be correlated to content, such as "It makes me angry when you break an agreement" instead of "You're an idiot." Words or actions can be fairly complained about. But character-assassinating words are harmful and never justified. If they happen, try to ignore them. Defending your character is pointless. Character is exhibited through action. It can't be defended with words. If your behavior needs improvement, you can make that improvement, or commit to making it.

If your lover is upset, that means an emotion is dominating the moment. Defending yourself blocks emotion from coming out. That emotion needs to come out. You are better off if it does. Expression releases tension.

You may have to withstand accusation or blame as your partner's hurt is vented. But you can guide the interaction toward uncovering that deeper hurt. By finding out the "I" instead of the "you."

Connor: "You don't love me anymore."

Austin: "Yes I do!"

The problem is an automatic defense is not enough. It doesn't address what is being felt by a lover. Like character, love is demonstrated through actions. Words mean less.

I will caveat that by saying some words, if effectively expressed, can be felt by a lover. If Austin loves Connor, he would be hurt by Connor's words. Austin could reveal that hurt.

Alternatively, Austin could draw upon his *feeling* of love to sing a love song, or give a big kiss and hug. If Austin does not feel defensive, he can creatively express his good feelings towards Connor.

A vulnerable share or creative feeling might be difficult to come up with in a tense moment. That's what makes doing something anti-tense so useful. It diffuses the tension. And takes *far* less energy than trying to drag yourself out of a defense pit.

An easy way to constrain the difficulty level is noticing if your partner is making a "you" or an "I" statement. "I" means the statement is about your partner. Just take in, or revel in, the information.

"You don't love me anymore," however, is a you statement. It is making a claim. It is not expressing a feeling. Underneath, the feeling might be "I feel insecure." Guiding a partner back to their feelings takes the pressure off you. This direction leads to a conversation about why your lover feels insecure, and what can be done about it.

Not defending yourself in any way gives a lover an opportunity to express something that needs to be expressed. Witnessing that expression is a handy *demonstration* of love. Defending demonstrates dislike.

Attacking Back

Attacking back is the most intense form of defensiveness. A damaging counterpunch is necessary in the boxing ring when facing a worthy opponent. A verbal counterpunch is just as damaging. Emotional injuries sustained during a fight, however brief, can take a long time to heal, if they ever do. Deciding you will not be the one that counterattacks is a useful strategy, and also feels good, since it eliminates the potential anguish of regret.

Your lover will offend you or hurt you. Your body's self-defense mechanisms activate and urge you to vomit your offense back at your lover. The actual offense is what is going on in your head. Your own thoughts are causing the pain you feel. Your interpretation of your lover's words or actions leads you to blame them for your pain.

Vomiting out your pain offers relief for about ten seconds. But then you face a mess to clean up. In the heat of the moment, you don't realize the damage you are doing. Ten seconds of relief is not worth ten hours of makeup effort.

You can avoid the mess if you understand that the vomit in your guts was not put there by your lover. The emotional pain of a heated moment begins with the self. The fire you feel has been building up. It is you who stoked it.

Marley: "Could you press harder?"
Jayden: "Nothing is ever good enough for you!"
Jayden: "You're always late."
Marley: "You're always on my case!"

The urge to counterattack does not mean you should, or that it is the perfect time to do it. It means you have become emotionally sensitive. That is information for you. It is an ideal time to look at possible root causes of that sensitivity.

We are all susceptible to stress-induced anger, no matter how enlightened we think we are. Stress reduces our mental functioning, leading to erroneous deductions and poor decisions. So if stress is influencing you or your lover, pause the current interaction and reduce the stress, before you growl like a trapped Wolverine.

Stresses come in many forms, and I am not immune, even after a fabulous ten-year polyamorous relationship with my partner Cheryl, a competent, open-hearted, tantra goddess. On a lovely summer day, Cheryl and I planned to meet friends at Fossil Creek for an afternoon of swimming and sunning. When we got there, we could not find our friends, or a cell phone signal. We disagreed about what to do, but since I was driving, I drove off in search.

I could see Cheryl edging towards cranky. The sun was heating us up, and we needed the cool of the water. My stressed brain had not accurately heard what she had said. I thought it was a criticism.

I blamed her for the tension in the car. Her head drooped in sadness. That touched me, and after a brief discussion, I came to understand that she was not upset with me at all. In reality, she regretted that she had not insisted on a backup plan before we got out of cell range. That, and she was hot. I had misinterpreted her signals.

Blaming her for my discomfort had been without justification. That is usually the case when we feel that urge.

Making Assumptions

Assumptions are inventions of your mind, and can easily be inaccurate or judgmental. It is impossible to know perfectly what a partner thinks or feels. That is good! It makes your time together fresh.

The fewer assumptions you make, the more open your mind will be to the real person your lover is, instead of a made-up version. It helps keep the reality of you both the truest. And the most positive.

Assumptions are a temporary disconnect with your partner. Acting on an assumption locks in that disconnect. Your actions make no sense. We all want to be viewed with high esteem by our lovers. Acting on a negative assumption will feel like a slap in the face.

Imagine a pensive look on your lover's face. That could mean gas pain, a criticism brewing, or another political rant. "Uh-oh," you say.

"You don't want to go to the beach today?" your lover asks, since contemplating which beach to go to created the slight knit in their brow.

That may seem trivial, but what if you assume that your lover no longer loves you? Your mind looks for evidence to confirm it. That assumption creates its own confirmation, by making your behavior less loving.

A healthy life with your lover means you spend time apart, so a lot will be unknown about each other. Can you just be neutral? As in, not needing to know everything? Assume life is good, and everything is OK unless proven otherwise. Then nothing needs to affect your behavior unless a decision is needed.

You may have to make some decisions for both of you. After analysis, act on your best guess. If you use your best guess, there is no need to feel guilty if your decision turns out to be a loser.

If you have agreements, then it is best to live up to them. But there will always be situational details that are not covered. That is a moment when an analysis, or assumption, is needed.

Assumptions are vulnerable to overly positive or overly negative thinking. If you are in an overly positive state, such as flirting at a bar, your analysis will be suspect. You could act out what you wish to be true, or forget to analyze at all. An inaccurate assumption allows you to keep flirting and playing with sexual energy. You don't want to stop to check in with your partner. You have taken unilateral action, ignoring any warning signs.

On your way home, fear and guilt creep in. That's an indicator your analysis may have been faulty. You will suffer the consequences.

If you don't reveal how you played around at the bar, you have to keep a secret. Relationships suffer from secrets. They form a barrier to complete intimacy and create anxiety about how the secret might be accidentally revealed. I counsel erring on the side of revealing. If that ends the relationship, then better sooner than later. Risk is involved, but the reward is increased intimacy. Nobody is perfect. If your lover expects, or demands, perfection, that may be too much pressure to bear.

A positive use of assumption is to assume your lover knows, or will know, everything. Such an assumption can improve your behavior and lower anxiety.

The more revealing a couple is, the more accurate their assumptions about each other. They get better at understanding each other, and the reasons for their behavior. Every day is an opportunity to learn, but you will always be playing catch-up since partners sometimes don't know themselves what their real motivations are.

For sure, you will make inaccurate assumptions. But you can lessen conflict over consequences if you try not to defend yourself. There is no defense. Your assumption was inaccurate. Your partner is the judge of that. Admit that you were wrong and apologize.

Let the judgment in. It will allow you to make a better analysis in the future. Use the reminder of an inaccurate assumption to focus more on your partner's exact words. No more, no less. Go by that reality. You don't have to second-guess. Life is more relaxed that way.

When an assumption pops in, ignore it, confirm it, or get it disconfirmed. Then update your perspective. Watch out for the tendency to continue running the assumption in your head, even if disconfirming evidence is found.

Whatever story about your lover is running in your head, it is not completely accurate. Might as well laugh at yourself for that. What does that sidelong glance mean? Everything, and nothing.

Thoughts are more negative than positive on average, so assumptions also edge negatively. They need editing to reinforce a favorable view of your partner.

Rehearsing a Response

Long-Term Lover: "My sister Brit is going out on a first date tonight."

Brit's dating history is checkered, and you have opinions you have not revealed. Criticisms arise in your mind, and responses form. You hear your responses playing, instead of taking in what is said. Data is lost. The crucial point is not revealed until the end. Brit has admitted a weakness and is implementing a new method to select better. The rehearsed response will be inappropriate.

It's hard to release attachment to rehearsed responses, and not use them when nothing else is in your mind to stop you. Your words will thud, since they are not in sync with the most current moment.

Surprisingly, your lover might also be fed up with Brit, and want to trash her exactly as you do, but will shift to a defense of Brit if criticism comes from you. The complete picture emerges if given time. A lover's rant that matches your thoughts feels delightful to you, and that way you avoid becoming the target of agitation. Whew. Nothing was needed except listening.

Wait, and stay supportive, until a sharing moment is complete. Then it is your turn. Search inside for what you are feeling, and share that. If it takes a little while, that is OK. It takes practice to overcome habitual responses and find what is hiding underneath.

You might encounter the fear that there are no thoughts or feelings happening within. Your mind is frozen, or blank. I know all about that! As an introvert, I have felt shame for decades due to my slow responses. Eventually, however, I noticed that if I stayed relaxed, something would pop into my mind.

You might be acutely aware of your lover's attention on you. A self-conscious state will make you feel separate and isolated. Focusing on the pain of self-consciousness only makes it last longer. You can train yourself to re-attend to the emotional or verbal content your lover is expressing.

While you are waiting for your flow to return, relax, breathe, and smile. I see flow as a state of nonresistance. That is, I don't feel an internal resistance to the urge to express. When a flow response comes, it will feel authentic, creative, playful, and even confident.

If my response is not well received, I know I can fix that by apologizing, and trying again.

The more relaxed you are, the more likely that a useful, humorous, or creative response will pop. What is the worst that can happen if your mind is blank? You will miss an opportunity to speak. That is not a huge loss. You may be attached to specific thoughts and fear forgetting them if they are not let out—immediately!

I have learned that any specific thought is not that important. Thoughts are a bottomless resource. I like many of them and want to share them, or at least keep them. Most thoughts can be remembered for a while, even while a lover is speaking. If a cherished thought is forgotten, it can re-emerge, if the mind is relaxed.

If your memory needs help, record a note on your phone.

Your thoughts are seriously significant only to you. Very much less so to anyone else. Your lover may be blown away by one of your mental masterpieces, but will not remember it a week later.

What will be remembered is how the moment felt.

Blocking or Sidetracking with Content

I define "content" as words and their meaning. Content is the realm of the rational mind. When we speak or write, there is an element of both literality and expressive inflection; precise meaning, plus embellishment or emotion.

The ratio varies a lot. "Argh!" is emotional.

"Blue." Rational.

"I don't like blue hair." Combo.

A problem with communication between lovers is knowing what type of expression it is: rational, emotional, or a

confusing mix. I believe emotions, by definition, are irrational. Therefore, emotionally expressed words may not make
rational sense.

Or their sense could be unearthed, but only if there were
enough time and patience. As emotion rises, the polarization
of rational versus emotional increases. In my experience, a
rational response to emotion is aggravating or frustrating to
the person expressing the emotion.

This type of aggravation happens all the time. There is
a tendency for the rational-state partner to block emotional
expression by selecting specific words to sidetrack with.

Riley: "I can't stand blue hair!"

Taylor: "Did you know that blue hair fashion began in
the 18th century?"

If sidetracking or misdirecting is successful, the emotional charge is still present and unprocessed. The moment
will become awkward. Emotional expression is required for
mental health. The cost of blocking it is high, leading to disappointing looks and shut-down behaviors from the emotional partner, for hours, days, weeks, or forever.

Your lover will feel frustrated by sidetracking, and you
will miss the message. It is possible they were just getting
started. That the real nugget had not come out. The nugget
might have been influential enough to affect your understanding. It might have been an aha. But you kicked it to the
curb.

You might fear the nugget. But nuggets are salient,
whether you want them to be or not. If a lover's ex-spouse
was blue-haired at the time they delivered the divorce de-
cree, a ton of emotion is connected to that specific hair color.
Powerful feelings about blue hair are guaranteed to return.
Your responses can help, or further hurt.

Another sidetrack is to nitpicking technical accuracy.

Riley: "I can't stand black hair!"

Taylor: "Hair is never actually black. More of a dark brown."

It's hard to resist making technical corrections if one is in a rational state. But not recognizing this communication mismatch will turn diffuse emotional energy into frustration directed squarely at you.

Rationality and technical accuracy have their place, but not as blocks or side tracks. That is a shut down path.

Invalidating

What if your lover declares you did not think that thought, feel that emotion, or sense that sensation? Sounds crazy, but it happens all the time.

Jimmie: "I smell pizza."

Maria: "That's impossible. There isn't a pizza place within a mile of here."

The distance to a pizza place may be accurate. But is that the limit of possibilities? No. Perhaps a neighbor is having a pizza party. Denouncing the interior reality of a lover is an attack. It happens even more with emotional expressions.

Ivy: "I hate my sister!"

Burt: "Don't be ridiculous!"

A partner claims that the emotion of hate, toward a sister, did not happen. Invalidation means challenging the accuracy of what is inside a person's head. It's a huge mind fuck. A vigorous poke.

Breeze: "Chocolate makes me sleepy."

Jason: "Chocolate can't make you sleepy. It has too much theobromine."

This response conflates chemistry with experience. Denying a reported experience is a super–dead end. A slap in the face. The opposite of respect.

Experiences can be objectively inaccurate. Humans are often wrong when they assign cause from effect. Case in point: the Salem witch trials. On the other hand, personal experience is the evidence that people most believe in. That is human nature.

Eric: "I'm joining my Alien Visitors group out at Pyramid Point tonight."

Samantha: "Do you have a history of mental illness?"

No two partners will have the same beliefs or views of reality. There has to be some slack around this. Intimacy depends on it. During purely conversational moments, you can rationally discuss these differences of opinion, when identities are not threatened. But when passion or emotion is involved, something core is being expressed, so proceed gently. There is always a way to respond that increases connection without surrendering to an opposing view.

Eric: "I'm joining my Alien Visitors group out at Pyramid Point tonight."

Samantha: "Hmmm. It will be interesting to hear what happens."

It is ultimately self-defeating to extinguish a lover's enthusiasm. Lovers have to do that for themselves, if they choose to. It might take a long time, and it might never happen. You can only model something different or something you think is better. Invalidation is confrontational. Many studies have revealed that people's beliefs are *reinforced* by confrontation since it compels them to defend something entwined with their identity.

If you have the attitude that your lover is your equal, you will give respect. That is the most exciting, and least boring, form of relationship. Each partner is more expert at something than the other. A professional musician might know why musical notes have effects on mood, but his or her partner can feel those effects. Feelings would then be common ground. "That piece of music makes me sad" would be valid for both. Inquiry is most effective when directed toward experience. An experience can be shared, whereas beliefs seldom can be.

A slang term for invalidation is "gaslighting," derived from the 1938 play and 1944 movie *Gaslight*, in which a husband tries to drive his wife insane by disagreeing with simple observations, such as interior gaslights dimming and brightening. The motivations of the stage and movie villain are sinister. A non-sinister invalidation can be just as harmful.

There is no more basic foundation of trust than accepting the authenticity of what is in your partner's mind or heart. Partners do lie. And all lies are manipulation. You can keep your own counsel on that. But the point is to separate objective reality from your partner's reality-in-the-moment.

The more you invalidate, the more you take on responsibility for controlling the relationship reality and its emotional energy. That responsibility will become a heavy burden.

Crystal: "This grass is too wet."

Jade: "It's not that bad."

That's like saying, "I am the expert here. Your view of it is wrong. Just shut up and accept my authority."

What would be a "validating" response? Bend down, feel the grass, and say, "Yes, it's pretty wet."

One person views the grass as wet and annoying. The other as wet and refreshing. There is no right or wrong perception. After both perceptions are validated, the next move can be inclusive.

Jade: "OK. I think we should take our shoes off and enjoy the wetness. It could be refreshing."

Crystal: "OK, I'll try that."

Invalidating a perception is an instant stop sign. We need to feel what we feel and will resent our lovers if they don't let us. That freedom benefits both of us since it opens the door to the most possibilities.

When lovers attempt to be themselves, and you tell them *not* to, you imply that you don't like them. They will notice. The pressure is on you to get your innermost thoughts in sync with your outward behavior.

It is useful to not be irritated by the lack of objective reality expressed by a partner. There will often be something there that makes you want to pull your hair out.

I counsel this radical extreme: *Everything* your partner says is true. Throw objective truth out the window, at least temporarily. That creates safety for authenticity to be expressed. The full flowering of an expression is the priority, at first. Then acknowledgment. Denying, rejecting, or ignoring an authentic expression stuffs it, and blocks connection.

The "everything is true" practice is identical to the "yes, and..." prime directive of improv. Always go with what your improv partner gives you. You are on stage, and a character says "Let's sit on this couch." If you reply with "There is no couch," the scene ends. The audience groans. That is a lot of dead weight to carry.

If you say "OK," and pretend to sit, the scene continues. It is far more fun and gives you the chance to interact in a state of flow instead of resistance.

Scientific reality is objective. Interpersonal reality is subjective. Subjective reality can be bent in many ways. If bending leads to increased pleasure and happiness, then what is the harm? The point is to let go of attachment to objective reality when it interferes with connection. For example, one of the best moments I had with a devotedly spiritual lover was acting as if I was the Hindu god Krisha while we were having sex. My desire to have fun and pleasure overrode my exasperation with her New Age beliefs.

I understand that objective reality is essential and should be discussed, but there is a time and place.

If you're getting hot and bothered during a conversation, it has moved from the rational realm to the emotional realm. Recognize that, admit it, and reveal the stirred emotions, instead of attacking the validity of the word content.

When something your lover says or does disturbs you, your reaction is your responsibility. If you continue expressing disturbance, your lover will feel rejected. That becomes a turnoff for you both.

A habit of celebrating all aspects of your lover leads you both into a spiritual and sexual paradise.

Criticizing or Judging

A cranky response leaks out when we are not feeling our best. When the urge to smack down comes up, analyze your state of self-care. Get the water, food, or rest you need to calm your nerves.

Appreciate a lover's skills, interests, and desires as a first response. If you have a problem with that, ask yourself why. What part of you is being challenged?

Criticisms or judgments are just thoughts that pop into our minds. We can let them dissipate instead of speaking them. If spoken, the partner will feel shamed, and the flow between us will stop. That is because shame runs deep and is more harmful than both you and your partner may realize. Shame drives the authentic self underground. And it may later resurface as discontent associated with you.

The urge to criticize or judge is all about you, not your partner. Your partner feels fine doing their thing. If a partner asks for feedback, that is different. Evaluation like that is a service. The urge to speak when an opinion is not asked for is what distinguishes criticism from feedback. That pesky urge means your response is emotional instead of rational. Emotional = It's About You.

Most people don't realize how many ways they are critical or judgmental. Wording can be subtle. For example, "Why are you upset?" is a criticism. It's like saying, "Why are you breathing?" Emotional states are a normal part of life.

We sense each other's states, at least subconsciously. Those states are affected by the critical and judgmental thoughts swirling around in our minds. Our animal bodies reflect our states through body language.

"I'm so horny!" your lover exclaims with a gleam in their eye.

Do your eyebrows shoot up? Do your jaws clench? Do you look away, and sigh? If so, you have signaled your lack of enthusiasm. Your lover will see that and feel rejected.

Maybe your only thought was that it would be better to wait until after sunset. But it could be too late to salvage a sexy feeling. A pattern of blah responses to initiative can lead to discouragement and resignation. A supportive first reaction to initiative can make a huge long-term difference. Discussion or negotiation can dial it back afterward if needed.

Everyone has the right to speak up for what does not work for them. But boundaries can be wielded as weapons. It is very much about how boundaries are communicated. If you lash out with defensive anger, you can easily crush your partner, instead of just delivering information. The adrenaline rush of an internal disturbance causes you to forget the tenderness of your lover's ego.

Your lover can't read your mind, so will sometimes violate your boundaries. That is normal. Compassionately share what is up. Describe the thing that is not working for you and make an agreement about it. Otherwise, it is not fair to blame.

Jake: "Don't you know you should never leave a kitchen sponge in the sink!?"

Such an outburst had a buildup. Why wasn't the concern about sink management brought up earlier? That is on the criticizer. The same content can be delivered constructively.

Zachary: "I prefer to keep the kitchen sponge in the holder at the edge of the sink, to keep it cleaner. Is it OK if we agree to do that?"

If a lover feels criticized or judged, then believe them, instead of arguing. Your opinion of your innocence does not matter. Your words felt critical. That is your partner's reality. Accept that reality.

Judgment is often a parroting of culturally ingrained morality, which you may not believe in but couldn't stop yourself from spouting. I propose removing all moral judgments of your lover. That keeps you functioning in the nitty-gritty of the here and now, instead of some unobtainable ideal.

No one has a perfect moral code or follows one perfectly. Behavior is the only real description of anyone's code. If you seek to influence your lover, then have faith in the effect of modeling your own code.

If you notice you are feeling judged, share that with your partner, rather than letting it build up. The purpose of the sharing is to inform, not diss. If it goes well, you will both learn from each other.

Giving Advice or an Opinion

Expertise and life experience are great, and can add a lot to discussions, meetings, and parties. In relationships, however, communication happens in two directions, and each member of the pair bond is the most expert on themselves.

Over time, people get better at knowing and doing what works best for them. That same best, however, is often not the best for their partner. It's frustrating when you offer what you believe is the best, and it is resisted.

Erica: "How was your day?"

Michael: "I was feeling a bit sluggish."

Erica: "I keep telling you that a vegan diet is the best for energy."

Michael: "And I keep telling you it doesn't work for me."

Erica: "You haven't given it a fair trial."

Michael: "Yes I have."

In this example, a connecting question turned into an argument.

Rebuff, resistance, and rejection from your lover feel crappy. Try to view resistance as "just information." Sometimes it takes a few tries to tune in to your lover well enough to recognize a good time and place to communicate. Attunement takes patience. For sure, the more frustrated you get, the more entrenched in rejection your lover will stay.

That rejection can be a gift from a partner. They may act as a filter for your bullshit, since advice and opinion are often just a running of familial or cultural programming, instead of real understanding.

Or a lover may resist due to their own programming. Never give up trying to influence a partner to grow, but massaging resistance works far better than attacking it.

In my experience, communications with a lover are in a category by themselves. Intimate. Take a moment to shift out of business-as-usual mode and into intimate mode. Both of you will feel that difference.

An academic, business, or strong-opinion mode may interest your lover. But maybe not. Tune in to how your mode is being received. It might shut your lover down. Your savvy insights might be felt as bluster since they are not connecting to your lover's emotions or sensations.

Some partners double down at that moment, instead of slowing down or stopping. You fail if your delivery blocks your partner from receiving. Overriding a partner's signals is arrogance.

If your partner is speaking to you, it is not a sign to burst forth with your cherished views. Partners want their moment in the sun. They may be thinking out loud, trying to reach their own conclusion.

Advice and opinion should be consensual. At "Cuddle Party," a safe-touch gathering led by certified facilitators, we practice asking for permission and receiving a "no" in response. It takes several parties for most people to get comfortable with that no, but it can be done.

"Would you like my opinion?" Wait for an answer. If the answer is no, then don't give your opinion.

Part of knowing how to respond is classifying an interaction as intellectual, pragmatic, excited, playful, or emotional. If it's emotional, the only thing needed is presence. Just be with the emotional flow, so it can come out, find its fullness, and then recede.

Anything else is interference. No matter how much of an expert you are. No matter what training or expertise you have, it is not better than allowing partners to be themselves, to process their stuff, either through words or catharsis.

Have faith in your partner. Your support builds the self-reliance you probably prefer they have.

Insisting on Being Right

Within our minds, thoughts and feelings come and go. We let them. We know our minds can change, and that we can be wrong. But if we *speak* our words, they take on greater importance, and we attach our identities to them.

We expect our words to be accepted, agreed with, acknowledged, and celebrated. Not derided or dismissed. We don't identify ourselves as stupid. Therefore, we defend our words and actions.

Sage: "This plant is so beautiful."

Forrest: "Yes, it is, it's..."

Sage: "If that isn't a testimony for God's handiwork, I don't know what is."

Forrest: "I think it's more a testimony for the laws of physics. The five leaf pattern is generated by..."

Sage: "Just because you studied biology and physics in college doesn't mean you know more than me!"

Sage and Forrest could have shared a beautiful moment together. Forrest was in complete agreement about the plant's beauty, but praise was interrupted when Sage threw down a bold claim. Forrest's response was measured, but an opposing view.

A ton of emotion came up when Sages's words were contradicted. More emotion than just a simple disagreement would indicate. Whatever emotion was at the root, that emotion erupted as an attack.

A challenge to our words raises our blood pressure. Our minds get a signal that the need to defend our words or actions is serious. But one can decide the situation is not serious. Too much seriousness is a turnoff. Take a moment to slow down and breathe. Contemplate your attachment to your thoughts or viewpoint. Your lover is not you. That's a good thing. The difference between you generates energy, which is required for sexual attraction.

Rightness is like an investment that loses money as time passes. The sooner you recognize that the investment is losing, the less money you will lose. If you hang on to rightness, your responsibility grows, making the weight of the relationship heavier. Heaviness does not feel good. You will blame your partner for the extra weight.

Your partner will resent being blamed. Dropping the belief that your thoughts and words are perfect, immutable, and need defending is an easy way to avoid self-defeating predicaments.

What we say is often a parroting of our programming. And just as likely we resent that programming. However, if it spews from our mouths, we recognize it as part of our identity and feel compelled to back it up. We get angry with those who "force" us to back this programming up, since we don't like revealing our lack of maturity or independence.

Try to notice when you are not comfortable saying what you are saying and wish you had not said it. You can stop and take it back. Or apologize. Or reveal your embarrassment.

Who is right after all? A rational discussion of facts may reveal a truth if the relevant facts are available. That search can be fun and interesting. But "winning" is a dangerous goal when directed at a lover. It can feel like an attack.

Analyzing or Interpreting

When a lover is expressing a feeling or thinking out loud, they want to enjoy that. Analysis and interpretation take away that pleasure and substitute self-consciousness. Like whipping out a video camera and pointing the lens.

Darrel: "I can't wait to watch the Warriors/Cavaliers game tonight!"

Deliza: "What's the big deal about basketball?"

Everyone has an enthusiasm that can be deconstructed into oblivion. But oblivion is the opposite of enthusiasm. Analyzing is a rational activity. Emotions are irrational. The two approaches don't mix. Attempting to make a situation rational instead of emotional is an effective deadener. It is the essence of dull.

Instead of being uplifted by your partner's enthusiasm, you are stuck in your mind. Thoughts form instead of feelings. Thoughts, questions, analysis, and interpretation—as the mind analyzes, the feeling of the moment is lost.

Analysis is also a way of changing the subject. Of bringing someone down. Watch your partner's face the next time he or she is happy. Start asking lots of questions and observe a smiley face slowly droop.

The need to know why is just the tinny voice of ego. It is not your job to dissect your partner. By definition, dissection destroys the living creature. Keep the creature—the life of the moment—alive.

Angela: "That movie was so sad, I feel like crying."

Enrique: "Did you know that you often feel sad after movies?"

The response, "did you know...," is an analysis instead of a sharing. The respondent could have said, "yes, it made me sad too," then pause to feel that sadness. Or, "I could feel you getting sad during the break-up scene. That made me sad too, but also angry, because the justification was so flimsy."

If you can't transition to a feeling state from a mental state, ask yourself what is blocking you. You may be stuck in a limitation. Your strengths are great. But they are not all of you. You don't earn points for refusing to look at your limitations or weaknesses. Ask yourself, "Why could I not quite stay with connection?"

Lovers want us to play with them, make them hot, and love them. No amount of analysis will be better than that. Technically, there is no need to know why a partner is saying or doing something. If you focus on the words or feelings, an appropriate and authentic response will pop out of you.

When it is your turn, you get the chance to share your own experience. A partner may have beliefs you find weird or feelings that puzzle you. Just because they are different from yours, you don't have to destroy them. Beliefs and feelings come and go. They may not have much meaning. A lover's trust in you is very meaningful.

Placating or Patronizing

Your lover has introduced an uncomfortable topic, and you want to get rid of it, so you say something marginally agreeable that hides what you are really thinking. This technique drains away energy or importance.

If your only motivation is escape, however, then your words will come back to haunt you, since you may have given your lover a message you did not wish to send, or made an agreement you did not want to make.

People like to hear what they want to hear. Nothing is wrong with that during sex play. But placating is a problem when you're not in play mode. It's not a good relationship sign if partners fear speaking to each other. Over time, the gap between them widens, often to the point where it can't be closed.

Placating differs from creatively giving your lover supportive words if needed, since then you would be expressing love and care. Placating is a way to care for yourself instead.

Roberto: "Let's go shopping for a cooler on the way home."

Sylvia: "I think we should study online options first."

You may want more study, or you may want to never shop for a cooler. Maybe the cooler symbolizes your acquiescence to go camping. Inside, you wish the topic of camping would never come up again.

The problem is, it will come up again. And if you fear a topic, your partner will notice. You will lose respect. Eventually, you will be unable to placate your way out of the situation. The sooner an issue is dealt with, the better.

The original placating was pretending to be interested in camping in the first place. Pretending is different from being open to your lover's influence over you. Interest means you are titillated, instead of fearful.

It is annoying and confusing when you avoid sharing your authentic self. Your partner notices the mismatch between words and tone of voice or body language. For whatever reason, you can't face your partner honestly. You could hate the topic, or just be tired. But trying to placate your way out of it will not end well.

Placating equals lying.

You don't have to be absolute about this. Truth sharing requires discernment. But it is your responsibility to avoid leading your partner too far away from your authentic self. Here's a test: Imagine you are revealing something to your partner. Are you calm, or nervous?

If you're nervous, then what you're thinking about revealing is impacting your relationship and should be revealed. Share with as much grace as you can muster. You are the one who created your truth. Your partner is not to blame. So don't act as if you are blaming.

It's OK to reveal the difficulty you have with a topic, but facing it can't be put off forever. If you need to excuse yourself when that stressful topic comes up, then commit to a future time to go into it.

Authenticity leads to the most relationship clarity. There are a million reasons why someone would dodge the truth. And all are manipulative. It is your responsibility to be sustainably authentic and accept whatever outcome arises from that. In my experience, the more you can face things, the more respect you get from a partner.

Patronizing is reaching for some form of authority, or superior knowledge, whether you believe in its rightness or not, to escape the same uncomfortable situation. It can even be something just made up on the spot and expressed with condescension.

Antonio: "Let's go shopping for a cooler on the way home."

Philippe: "I guess you didn't read that article about the importance of getting a high-end cooler and packing it perfectly, to avoid salmonella poisoning. It's more complicated than you think."

Interrupting an Emotional Expression

Emotions are always building up for everyone, all the time, and it is essential for mental health to express them. The full expression of emotions is one aspect of "discharging," a term popularized by Harvey Jackins, founder of Re-evaluation Counseling, a peer-to-peer organization, and likely first applied to emotional process work by Wilhelm Reich in the 1930s.

Like a battery, discharging utilizes the buildup of energy. It is useful for relationships to allow as much emotional discharge to happen as needed, rather than blocking it until it overloads a circuit, meaning a fight.

It doesn't matter who is blocking whom. If emotional expression is self-blocked or partner blocked, kinetic energy converts to potential energy, and is stored in the limbic system, under the category of "lover," or "partner."

Discharging allows a flow of emotional energy to hit its peak, draining off what has built up in storage. In my experience with relationships, that is a good thing.

This is a common scene: A cisgender couple are in bed caressing. The woman is tired from a day's work, and welcomes this chance to feel better. She starts to relax and feel her body's sensations.

The man is tired too, so is not bubbling with confidence. "Maybe we should just go to sleep now," he says.

"OK," she replies. However, she is disappointed. She wanted to spend more time in pleasure.

He is also disappointed. He was hoping she would say "This is feeling great! Can we continue?"

A chit of disappointment is added to the emotional energy bank of both partners, and there is no plan to discharge it. The emotional charge is stored in the hippocampus, amygdala, hypothalamus, and other limbic brain regions.

Emotional energy can be represented visually as a wave. The elements of a wave are frequency, amplitude, and wavelength. Frequency is how often the wave happens. Amplitude is the height of the wave, measuring its intensity. Wavelength is the time span of a single wave.

The total amount of energy in need of discharge is the area under the curve of the wave. The higher the amplitude (intensity), the shorter the wavelength (how long it takes).

Did I just say the intensity of emotional expression correlates with how long the expression lasts? Yes, I did. The fullest expression is the most time-efficient.

Within most social settings, intense emotional discharge is frowned upon. That may also be necessary for the smooth functioning of organizations. Discharge is, therefore, a personal endeavor which lovers can facilitate for each other, at home.

That may not sound like your thing, I know. Many unhappy prior experiences trained most of us to avoid emotional situations. We default to every kind of blocking behavior we can think of.

We block the teeniest hint of emotion out of fear that it will grow into a tidal wave and we will drown. That fear stems from a lack of experience and understanding. Every wave has to obey the laws of physics. It will recede. The only challenge is how to swim in the wave.

Resistance to an emotional wave acts like a breakwater, increasing the height of the wave and creating interference peaks before the wave achieves enough amplitude to breach the wall.

It doesn't matter what emotional situation generated the wave. Even if you are being attacked or blamed. The irony is that if you don't resist it or block it, the wave recedes on its own.

Imagine our basketball-watching couple has settled in for a Warriors/Cavaliers game. The camera zooms in on an attractive woman. Without even realizing it the man exclaims "Hot!" His lover gets pouty and turns silent.

How does he handle this situation? Apparently, his lover has had a jealousy response. He could withdraw into silence, filled with feelings of guilt or shame. The silence showdown could last for a few minutes, or days.

He could get annoyed and express his displeasure. "It's just a chick on TV. What is your problem? Don't ruin the game, OK?" He thus attempts to wipe out his partner's buildup of emotional energy. Would that work?

Nope. The game is already ruined. He realizes this and switches to understanding. "Hey babe, sorry my comment upset you. Would you like to speak about that?"

If his lover gets to "discharge" her jealousy wave, then the air is cleared. His encouragement may allow *her* to hear the depth of her complaint. Letting that out is cathartic. He doesn't have to agree to any behavior change, just listen.

The jealousy moment has to be handled. Airing it out can provide a movement toward personal growth for her. It begins subtly, gains steam, peaks, then tapers off. That discharge peak is then complete. There may be several waves or peaks. But eventually, the jealousy charge is dissipated. It runs out of steam. That is the way all living beings are made, like an antelope shivering after being chased by a cheetah.

It's the only way it can go well. The man sacrificed the game to be present for his woman. Her emotional wave passed before the game ended, and they returned to watching while snuggling closer.

You may say to yourself that there is no time in your modern life for even one tiny bell curve of emotional expression. Time constraints are real. But time is also used as an excuse to avoid emotional expression altogether.

The reality is, emotions have to be acknowledged in some way. And the best way is the easiest way. Surprisingly, the more space for discharge you give, the less involvement you have with your lover's emotional outbursts. What? Yep, resistance is involvement. It adds energy to the peaks, like an interference wave. Presence, or compassion, is just observing. Like watching a movie.

If you cry with your partner, empathetically, isn't that involvement? Nope. You are simply allowing your partner to affect you, as if you were the molecules of moisture carried within in a cyclone.

I understand how scary, or uncomfortable, emotions can be. In spite of that, emotions come up in response to something almost every day. A lover's glance that you can't interpret. Being called into your boss's office.

If you are honest with yourself, don't you get a twinge of emotion every day with your partner? A tickle of love, or a twist of anger. Emotions in a relationship are inescapable, short of breaking up. The logical thing to do is get better at them.

Look at emotions as part of normal life. You can begrudge the need to shop for food and cook it. Or you can delight in deciding what to make, choosing the freshest-looking produce, and putting your spin on the recipe.

Your lover is a meal in the making. Accept the need to eat and make the best of it. When your lover brings you an emotional meal, sit down and relish it. If you do, you will feel more of life than you thought possible.

You may think the ravenous need for emotional expression is unjustified. I know how frustrating it can be when you don't understand why some issues are a big deal. Sorry, but you'll have to work on that. Your frustration does not help your lover.

Accept that there are valid reasons for an emotional buildup, and practical if flawed reasons the buildup has not been dealt with. Frustration acts as resistance and adds fuel to the emotional fire. Support releases that frustration. If you are not in reaction, then you keep yourself out of the emotional energy system. You don't add to the total energy under the wave.

That way, your partner is responsible for the time spent in discharge. If you are not trying to be the controller, it's easier for you. You can release that responsibility. Whew!

Here is a mind-blowing irony: The less you try to control a lover's emotional expression, the more control you have. When the feelings of the moment are revealed, all the mystery or confusion evaporates. The more you know, the more you can be effective.

Giving your partner full responsibility for their emotions is the most reliable path to your partner's long-term mental health since your partner will be less subject to your unintentional mind fucks. A mentally healthy person will want that responsibility.

Give responsibility, but offer support. How do you know when support time is over? Reading emotional energy is an art. It takes practice. Start with observables: rate of breath, depth of breath, face flush, body language, a sigh of relief, a lull. If you make a move toward completion, and meet resistance, then that was too soon.

You can learn to be graceful about it. You are not the "decider." Your lover is done emoting when it feels complete. Manage your self-care *and* learn to have more patience and endurance. Try to remember that the more supported a lover feels, the more quickly they will be complete, in minutes, or years.

The most significant issues take the longest. Cheryl still has jealousy reactions after ten years with me, but the total upset energy load has been reduced by 90 percent.

Patience with a partner's process is rewarded more and more over time. It may seem like emotional needs are never-ending. One has to have faith. More time, at first, may be needed to clear the backlogs.

With the right attitude, supporting partner discharge is pleasurable, entertaining, and can lead to sex. If they feel supported, they are grateful and want to give back.

Resistance to a partner's emotional expression ensures the opposite effect. Instead of being discharged, the emotional backlog gets directed at the resistor. Gratitude, and the possibility of sex, will not be forthcoming.

I used to hate emotions and was only in resistance to them. But with education, I came to realize that I felt better when I revealed them. That understanding led me to be more accepting of the emotions of others. Facilitating emotional processing even became my profession.

It was a relief to gain skills and embrace emotions as a positive instead of a negative. Amazingly, it takes zero energy to flow with emotions instead of blocking them. I no longer resent the time spent riding those waves. It's more engaging than TV and offers many possible pleasures.

An emotionally connected, supportive interaction makes people feel good, like being in love. When lovers feel good, they want to enjoy their partners sexually.

To stop fighting, the first step is not poking a lover's bear, as described in this chapter. Many lovers are not aware of the ways they poke. But the results are observable. When a lover is not responding well to you, it's time to check the list from this chapter.

A long-time lover may have suppressed negative reactions so well that they are hard to observe. In that case, it will be more up to you to notice if interactions are connecting or not. Tune in to your senses as much as possible, to detect the tiniest of details.

If interactions are problematic, pain or discomfort should arise within you. That pain is a blessing, not a curse. It's the perfect motivator for constructive action. Let pain whisper in your ear, like a relationship coach that never leaves your side.

4

Taming the Bear

Charlie Vandergaw, "The Man Who Lives with Bears," has never been injured, even after forty-five years of living with bears in a remote area of Alaska. He overcame his instinctive fears and learned the bears' communication cues, so he could play and cuddle with his wild friends.

Theoretically, humans should be able to communicate with each other as safely as Charlie does with grizzlies. Unfortunately for sexual partnerships, that is not the case. When sensitivities activate uncontrollable reactions, the jaws of emotion open wide and have the urge to bite.

All of us feel emotions every day. We like some emotions, but hate others. We cling to the importance of our own emotions and discount those of everyone else. Denying our self-centered emotional focus is a recipe for disaster.

No matter how good a relationship is, something uncomfortable will come up between the partners. A look, a sound, a request, a desire, a plan, a creative thought, an intense feeling—because partners are different human beings, they will set each other off.

Whether you are prepared or not, you have then entered the realm of emotions. You don't have to reject that world out of fear. You can explore the emotional jungle, with some guidance.

Emotions are natural. There is no need for shame. Emotions just arise in our brains, like thoughts. Some emotions hurt. Evolution gave us this pain so we would do something about it.

Laughing, discussing, playing, and teasing are all good. But pay attention to the moment when something shifts. Your lover looks bothered. Apparently, you have poked your lover's bear. This is an important realization. It allows you to shift from poking to soothing. The fun you were having will return if you connect with their emotional state instead of rejecting it.

Rejecting a lover's emotional state tells their limbic system that you are not safe. Connecting, on the other hand, builds in extra "slack" or "ease" that comes in handy when you are the one needing support.

You can pop into compassion or empathy, much like "unconditional positive regard," a term used by clinical psychologists. You might be thinking, "I have to be a psychologist?" Don't worry. I am presenting a consumer version that students and clients have been able to learn.

You also might be thinking you don't have time for it. It's true that giving space to emotions may take more time at first. But at some point, the backlog will get used up and you'll both realize you've become more chill. Not to mention happy.

When you are overwhelmed, angry, and resentful toward a partner, you may seek to strike it from memory and hope it never happens again. But it will. And there you'll be, still on the same sinking ship.

Most heterosexual men feel lost at sea when emotional waters get choppy. Their women ache for a captain who knows what to do instead of diving overboard. Women are sensitive to these moments and may shut down sexually if their emotions are rejected. Even if they don't want to.

A different approach is the only way back to land. That approach will take time to learn, but the payoff is enormous. It's like becoming a new head football coach. Rebuilding a losing team takes effort and dedication. The turnaround is not noticeable at first. But in the third year, the team makes a run at the national title, like the 2016 Washington Huskies.

The team reestablishes itself as a national power and can focus more on fine-tuning, instead of fundamental problems. Healthy people want to be self-reliant and win championships. They tire of hearing themselves speak about the same issues over and over and decide to do something about it. In the meantime, some metaphorical gritting of teeth may be required.

Giving space to emotions saves time in the long run. It allows relationship snafus to progress instead of staying stuck. A few minutes of feeling heard is like a love shower. We crave that from our lovers.

Conveniently, love is an action, not just a feeling. The captain gives the love order. The act of love, via the skills described in this chapter, becomes a feeling of love. If you *do* love, your inner self catches up with your behavior. You have then manipulated yourself into a better state. Action transforms powerlessness into power.

You never again have to wonder what to do.

Responses That Disarm and Reconnect

- Breathe and Be Patient
- Pleasant Body Language
- Put Ego on Pause
- What Are You Afraid Of?
- Self-Soothing
- Adjust Expectations
- Notice Key Words and Phrases
- Identify the Emotion
- Inquiry That Goes Deeper into Feelings
- Empathize
- Provide Physical Comfort
- Be Encouraging and Supportive
- What Are You Vulnerable About?
- Apologize and Make Up
- Learn by Trial and Error

Breathe and Be Patient

An easy first response to a lover's emotions is: Breathe. The instinct to breathe deeply as a way to cope can become automatic. The body can learn to react this way, without thinking. You get help without even trying.

The drama of emotions emits a lot of energy. Bodies feel the impact. Deep breathing tells the body that everything is OK. If the body feels OK, it doesn't have to move into a defensive posture, which could lead the mind into defense too.

A non-reactive body/mind can then track a lover's emotions. The deeper you breathe, the more you can keep your emotional reactions separated from your partner's. Awareness of the sensations of breath reinforces your sense of being a whole, complete human, who has a life parallel to, but not the same as, your lover's.

The last chapter posited that you are not responsible for your lover's emotions. The flip side of that is that you *are* responsible for *your* emotions, no matter what emotional ups and downs your lover is experiencing. Take in your responsibility as you breathe.

The first few seconds are more important than you realize. They set the stage for the course of the interaction. The initial goal is to not get wiped out by a spike in emotional drama—yours or your lover's. You *can* survive without defending yourself or attacking back. Breathing can be a key that reminds you that you don't have to know anything other than a human limbic system has felt threatened.

The first level of survival is handling the energy "punch." For sure, your body takes a hit. But you can train yourself for that. A wave of emotional energy coming at you is just sound and light. Your body can handle it. The real impact is in your mind.

The situation compares well to boxing. Showtime's *Masters of Sex*, based on the lives of ground-breaking sex therapists and researchers, William Masters and Virginia Johnson, is one of the best TV shows ever. In Season 2, Episode 3, the colleagues/lovers are spending the night in a hotel room. A championship boxing match is on the black-and-white TV in the background, but discussing the match gets Bill to reveal his past with his abusive father.

Bill became a master at absorbing punches, similar to the reigning boxing champ, Archie Moore. Ginny complains that a punch-absorption strategy is masochistic. Bill replies that you stop feeling it after a while. In the case of Bill's father, Bill could not control the timing of a violent outburst, so instead learned to control his reactions to them.

In Bill's story, a child gets pounded by an adult. The child Bill appears powerless, but he is not. In a boxing ring with matched fighters, overreacting to punches is a significant flaw. It uses up energy and reveals a lack of skill. Supreme defensive boxer Floyd Mayweather reigned as champ for a decade and was seldom hurt. He understood that the attacker's arms (the emotional outburst) will wear out, allowing him to take control in later rounds.

Deep breathing is like bobbing, weaving, and slipping punches in the ring, and barely noticeable to a lover. Simultaneously, one can scan the rest of one's body for muscles that have tensed up, paying particular attention to abs and shoulders. Try to relax those muscles.

Next, notice the overall position of your body. Is it stiff, or angled away from your partner? Make yourself more comfortable. Unfreeze your movements. Use body language to signal to yourself and your partner that everything is OK. That the challenging interaction is not life-threatening, just a few rounds in the gym.

Breathing deeply also reminds you to slow everything down, and allow your lover to complete expressing, before you respond in any manner. Breathing helps you connect to your patience.

Patience is merely having some control over your ego. Your mind (ego) is saying "Me, Me, Me! I want to speak!" Or "This sucks!" The problem is your lover will not hear you, and will feel attacked if you jump in before an expression is complete.

Patient breathing may be all you need to do to support your lover. What could be easier? Your lover expressed something, you listened, and the moment is complete. You can let it go. Some sensations were felt, and thoughts were thought, but you both will be OK. On the other side of stress is relief. Enjoy it.

If the interaction demands more time, patience can lead to vulnerable sharing, which is infinitely better than an exchange of nasty attacks. Vulnerable sharing is deliciously intimate.

Patience is like pushing the slow-motion button. It gives you more time to deal with the word content of emotional expression. You need as much patience as possible, since the word content may be challenging. It may freeze your brain.

What happens to you if your lover asks you about a handwritten note containing the name and phone number of someone you are flirting with? Most likely, you will give away your guilt. However, you can recover, and proceed to a vulnerable form of revealing, if your body isn't freaking out. That gives your brain a much better chance of emotionally intelligent operation. Not blaming your lover for what you are feeling, for example.

You might think that freezing up or getting tense, leading to a defensive attack, is the most authentic response. I would agree, in situations of physical danger. But your lover's emotions are only dangerous to *your* emotions. And emotions reflect only a percentage of the complete self. From moment to moment it is possible to switch from love to hate, and back again. Each emotional moment is only partially meaningful.

The bodily sensations of tense situations can feel very uncomfortable. The mind and body hate them. If you like something, you want it to continue. If you don't, you want it to stop. Your lover can see your dislike and feel rejected. So a habit of patience as a first response gives your body a chance to moderate its responses.

One can learn to moderate bodily reactions through controlled exposures, like easing into a frozen lake, for example. I'm no Wim Hof, cold-water immersion record holder, but I've been able to reach the point of hypothermia pass-out in the Breitenbush River, Oregon, after heating up in a 108-degree hot tub. My trick is to dissociate from skin sensation, since core temperature takes a while to drop. Eventually, the core gets cold, but in a stimulating and refreshing way. Popping back into hot after that is a tingly pleasure.

A wave of emotional energy can be an icy threat to normal body functioning, but the body can likewise be trained to radically delay its response.

Pleasant Body Language

You arrive home from work and see your partner sitting on the couch with a serious expression on their face. You feel a twinge of apprehension. As you walk over, your partner looks up and says "I have something to tell you."

Do you stop in your tracks? Or get a stab of pain in your guts?

A fear response to such words causes physical changes throughout your body. Your lover sees these changes and is discouraged. Rejection anxiety rises for your lover, who wanted to tell you something important, such as getting a job offer in a different city. A delicate communication is teetering on the brink of disaster within milliseconds.

Fear and apprehension create a wall of separation between you and your lover. Relaxing tense muscles can counter this instinct. It will appear as though you are still OK, even if your guts are roiling.

The purpose of controlling your body language is to delay reactions long enough to gain more information. To find out what the whole story is before formulating your response, since initial responses can so easily be wrong.

A large portion of body language–speak is sent via the face, particularly the eyes. Looking away can be an indicator of fear, anger, disgust, or dislike. Maintaining eye contact, while relaxing facial muscles, counters that disconnect. Extend that relaxation down into your abdominal muscles. Breathe fully into your diaphragm and belly, stretching the abs instead of contracting them. Deeper breathing reduces the pain of challenging emotional content, so you can stay functional. So you don't misclassify rapid sensation upticks as signals of enormous meaning.

Your body position, relaxed demeanor, and gentle touch emphasize what you say with your eyes. What will your lover feel when looking into your eyes? If your mind is peaceful, and your face relaxed, you can communicate "positive regard," even if you feel shaky. With practice, you can learn to default to receiving words or emotional expressions positively, at least on the surface. This default will keep you going until your heart catches up, or the moment eases.

The time spent observing and listening to a challenging story from your lover will be longer than you wish. But you can get something from that time. Sitting, breathing, and gently looking into your lover's eyes is—drum roll please—Tantra, the ritualized practice of sacred sexuality developed in ancient India. Viewed this way, resentment over time or effort spent can morph into a transcendental experience.

You might not be able to use words, but just sitting together is an act that demonstrates togetherness at a primal level. Your animal bodies have gotten used to each other, so togetherness is a counter to the fear of separation. It only takes a few seconds to move in closer.

That is a physical demonstration of the desire to stay connected, no matter what your lover is doing. Calmed bodies can listen more effectively and take in what is being shared. Your heart might be touched by closeness, which feels lovely to both of you.

Part of resistance to listening is the fear of being affected by content. It might challenge self concepts. That's scary, but a gift of relationship.

Fear is natural, but it is the "mind killer." Unfamiliarity can stimulate that fear. If part of your identity wavers, that can feel deadly serious. You might have the thought "You will not change me, no matter what."

Change is optional, of course. But it is useful to credit your lover's input. To at least not reflexively reject it. Patience helps you remember: "I am not now, and never will be, perfect. And I don't have to be. My partner loves me anyway."

The practice of Pleasant Body Language forces you to counter defensive actions, increasing your chances of surviving an emotional energy rush, and converting it into a significant intimacy event.

Your lover is not the threat. The actual danger is your ego. Something has come up that threatens your ego, and that is scary. But if the relationship is stuck, genuinely seeing each other can lead to needed changes.

Put Ego on Pause

Even if you have controlled your body enough to appear relaxed after something scary has come up, your mind might scream "Run!" Or an uncooperative "Fuck that." There is an urge to repeat such thoughts to yourself, louder and louder.

This is the choice point, where you request that your primitive self calm down. It will resist because it claims to be your true self. But your true self is more complicated and variable.

A looser view of yourself will not be rigidly attached to a specific identity. You can put yourself on "ego pause," as we say. The purpose of ego pause is to give you time to take in more data, with an unobstructed view. It gives you time to remember that your partner is not your enemy.

And, perhaps, making a good point. Your partner may be right about some weakness you have. That hurts a lot. You don't want to have any defects. But you do. Your partner also wants you to be your best. The suggestion on offer might make you a better person.

Admitting all of that can be hard. But the intensity of the moment is useful for change. Use the moment to work on yourself, real-time. It is the ultimate in efficiency. See if it is possible to create an impartial perspective to view input, in place of automatic or legacy reactions.

I have a great relationship with my primary partner, Cheryl. We enjoy modeling the ego-pause principle during classes, or in sessions with couples. We were teaching a class called "Your Emotions Make Me Hard!/Wet!" at a fabulous hot springs resort, when Cheryl blurted out "I want you to be a bigger man!"

I could hear the class hush into silence. I was silent too, for a moment. Cheryl surprised me with a classic challenge to my male ego. A perfect test for my ego-pause state. In pause, I waited for my response. I knew it would come.

I rose to my feet, stood tall, spread my arms wide, and loudly exclaimed, "I will be a bigger man from now on!"

As affirmatively as possible, I expressed my acceptance of Cheryl's challenge. Following through on it would be good for me. I wanted to get bigger too. My male ego did not block this precious moment. The effect has been positive for us both.

Women have egos too. They feel threatened by a different set of factors, but the ego-pause principle works the same for all genders. The quieter the ego, the more open lovers are to their fullest functionality. It's a win-win.

Your agenda, beliefs, habits, and thoughts are not relevant to the full acceptance and appreciation of your lover's emotional expressions. For that moment, you are just the stage upon which their performance is being played. A competing or controlling ego detracts from that moment. Your partner will love you for expressing empowering regard instead of continual limiting.

What Are You Afraid Of?

Fear is a gift, and your partner is the giver. When fear comes up, it is time to look within and ask what you are afraid of, instead of squashing the bringer of fear.

Specific fears are correlated with lovers. The fear of loss is a big one. Your status is perhaps lower than you believed. (Loss of your reality.) A weakness might be exposed. You could be embarrassed. You may be ashamed of your true identity.

Your sexy self-identity seeks to defend itself. It wants to see the look of desire in a lover's eyes. In reality, identity is fluid. How hot you feel varies a lot, independent of the presence of your lover.

If you are in a state of fear, your partner will see it, since you will exhibit fearful behavior. The truth already exists. To admit it brings it out into the open, where it can be soothed.

The fear of change or loss is physically painful. Nature gives us this pain to motivate action. But a lack of relationship skills inhibits change and increases the likelihood of loss.

It's human nature to remember instances of emotional pain more than pleasure, so we carry sensitivities into any new relationship. Few of us heal and gain permanent new skills after a relationship breakup, so our familiar fears are ready to resurface.

But we need to remember that our fears are our own shit. We had them before we met our partners. Our lovers will, justifiably, not appreciate getting blamed for them. When the urge to blame rises up, look inside for the fear within you.

Expressing your most crippling or annoying fears with a confidant, or therapist, goes a long way toward overcoming them. You are responsible for finding that resource. Your lover may listen to some fears, but never all.

Your lover will be open to listening depending on how vulnerable and non-blaming you are. Vulnerable revealing means describing thoughts or feelings in a way that does not push responsibility onto your partner. Requesting, or hoping, that a partner will take care of your issue is just whining. You don't get any points for that.

Speak the fear, such as "I'm worried that you want to spend less time with me," then stop. The fear is exposed. That helps to ease your burden. Hopefully, your lover can hear that compassionately. But a lover is not required to do anything other than witness your feelings.

A discussion regarding the amount of time to spend together may ensue. The more you learn about each other, the more you can come to a non-threatening compromise.

Self-Soothing

Consider taking responsibility for *everything* that you think, say, feel, and do. That could seem like too much responsibility. It could feel overwhelming. On the other hand, it could be empowering. If we are victims of our mind movie, then we are less likely to take action.

I'm not saying we should be responsible for everything that happens to us, in a New Age, karma way. We are born with genetic tendencies, such as a higher risk for cancer or Alzheimer's. And we don't have control over people who might drive a car into us, or rob us.

I'm also not saying we are responsible for generating the thoughts and feelings that pop into our heads. But we *are* responsible for managing our thoughts and feelings, no matter what our lovers say or do, short of physical violence.

To enhance survival, evolution has given us a bias toward negative interpretations of our surroundings. The modern world has minimized the need for that bias. We can remember that and use our minds to tell ourselves a safer story.

We can forgive our crazy impulses, calm our nerves, and replace negative thoughts with positive ones. "I'm OK" can be a go-to mantra, instead of "This sucks," or "I'm out of here."

When Cheryl challenged me in class, I could have collapsed. I could have thought, "How could she do this to me?" But a more fun thought is "Wow, that was a good one!" Cheryl and I purposely try to trigger each other live so we can demonstrate how our teaching principles work. I knew what Cheryl meant by "bigger." Compared to her, I was less out in the world creating something.

At first, I went blank. The class was waiting to see how I would respond. I observed myself sitting there, but I wasn't triggered. Meaning I was not debilitated. I knew I would be OK. That an acceptable response would appear within me. This flow of thoughts and feelings lasted about two seconds. Then my response happened.

It went over well for the group, for Cheryl, and me. Excuses have blocked my bigness forever. But here was a moment when that could change, and I took it. I took in the pressure on me to work on myself, real time. It didn't matter in what way I would become bigger. I was just announcing that I was doing it.

Because I have the habit of "self-soothing," a practice described by David Schnarch in *Passionate Marriage*, I kept my fears at bay. Micro waves of anxiety came and went. In the subsequent emptiness, a successful response burst open. The state of emptiness filled itself—with something other than compulsive repetition of negatives.

There is no time when repetitive negative thinking is better than self-soothing. This is particularly true in bed with lovers. If a man fears he won't get hard, or will come too soon, those outcomes are more likely to happen. If a woman fears she will not get wet, or take forever to come, ditto.

With practice, you can develop a self-soothing "go to" groove. For sexual insecurities, I have trained myself to re-focus on the sensations of pleasure in my own body, and my lover's. This technique was introduced as "sensate focus" by Masters and Johnson in their 1970 book *Human Sexual Inadequacy*.

Resetting focus to sensate has worked enough times that I no longer worry. Persistent sexual and emotional issues may need discussion or therapy, but some method of self-soothing is handy as a first response.

Adjust Expectations

Expectations are a shortcut to reduce the workload of our brains. We expect the sun to come up, so we don't waste time on it. This process also occurs while collecting data on your lover. Your brain can't take in all the information presented, so it ejects what it can't store. Therefore the mental image of your lover might never be more than 50 percent accurate.

For this reason, your partner says and does things that don't match your expectations. This can be jarring, confusing, and even enraging. Nature doesn't care that our minds create inaccurate pictures of our lovers under the influence of dopamine. When dopamine wears off, we expect our partners to make it flow in our blood again, and are irritated when they can't. When they diverge from perfect supportiveness.

But it is not your partner's job to meet your expectations. At least if the expectation is not the keeping of an agreement. Agreements are a way for expectations to align. When behaviors clash, then discussion leading to negotiation, leading to an agreement, is a comforting and encouraging outcome.

Without a conscious effort to update each other, lovers expectations are out-of-date. An open mind is needed. Each day is an opportunity to learn something new about the real lover in your life.

Your lover will change. That is a given. You may be attached to the way your lover was in the past. That will only cause you pain. The spontaneity of the present can make up for your loss.

There's no need to beat yourself up for having expectations. They pop into the brain, like thoughts and feelings. But expectations run with momentum, like a flash flood, so they may be a challenge to redirect.

Imagine your lover comes home one day, enthused about skydiving. They want to try it this weekend and want you to do it too. You had expected to catch up on weeding.

How can you respond other than "No way!"?

You could be evasive. "That skydiving company only gets a four-star rating."

Or invent an artificial barrier. "I think my toe hurts too much."

The real reason for your lack of enthusiasm could be yard shame, money shame, or a fear of heights.

How do you handle a partner's disruption of your plans? Start with something positive.

"What an amazing idea!" Supportive, but not an agreement.

Then gently bring in your authentic resistances if they are vulnerable. That can bring out your lover's compassion.

"On the other hand, I'm behind on yard work."

The state is now neutral. Plans for the weekend are up for negotiation, which can lead to an agreement, leaving you both in alignment. That feels good.

You may have resistance to negotiation with your partner, but accepting negotiation as a frequent and normal activity is very helpful. If the thought of changing your plans is upsetting to you, that is useful information about yourself.

You can investigate why particular desires or plans of yours are sacred to you. Revealing that sacredness or passion to your partner may sway the negotiation. I submit, however, that being open to negotiation is more valuable than attachment to a specific outcome.

What happens to your mind and emotions when your lover does not match your expectations is all about you. If you are angered or annoyed, that is on you. It is just in your head. There is no meaning to it. It is only a reality reset.

Notice Key Words and Phrases

You don't have to listen to every word. Just the important ones. For example, your partner could tell you about a friend with relationship problems. You observe that your partner feels sad for the friend. Sad may be the only word you need to remember. What does sad need? Comfort. Your partner's friend is not the content. Your partner's sadness is.

Neither of you can fix the friend. But you can help with your lover's sadness. Respond to sadness with comfort until the sadness is complete or has transitioned to another emotion or another subject. That is a success.

If you are not interested in your partner's friend's relationship problems, then don't return to that subject. It is over and gone.

Observe the new emotion or topic, and flow with that. Little effort is needed. You can coast along until a new topic lights you up, or it is your turn to share what's up with you.

Lovers feel loved if you tune in to what they value as important. When your lover takes the floor, let their words fill your mind. What you value is temporarily put aside. Acknowledging key words and phrases demonstrates your understanding of a partner's values.

When a lover receives support for what is important, they feel empowered, energetic, and uplifted. If you are helping the uplift, then a joyful feeling is associated with you. A credit goes into the limbic system experience bank.

The Center for Nonviolent Communication, at https://www.cnvc.org/Training/feelings-inventory, provides a detailed list of words that indicate feeling states and how they relate to values and needs. A lover's words can be a window into a lover's soul, if you can hear them.

How do you acknowledge key words and phrases? The easiest way is to display a reaction via words like "Wow!" accompanied by facial expressions, and body language. The response depends on the topic. If a partner requests help to prepare a potluck dish, then be ready when the time comes, and be as helpful as possible.

Sometimes one has clarify what is important.

Spouse: "We have to leave in five minutes. Are you sure you want to wear that shirt?"

What is the most important point, or points within these statements? Is the focus on how little time there is? How solid the shirt selection is? Or is the speaker apprehensive about making a request to change the shirt selection? How does this couple handle a little rise in tension, and make it a win/win, within five minutes?

You: "Are you nervous about the time?"

Spouse: "Not really." Cool, let that go for a moment.

You: "Are you unhappy with this shirt?" Ask as neutrally as possible.

Spouse: "It's not one of my favorites." Your lover has an opinion, but not a strong one.

You: "I like this shirt, but how important is it to you that I pick another?" Sharing an opposing opinion, then proceeding with further inquiry.

Spouse: "Medium." Clear enough for decision making, but for good measure, a final inquiry.

You: "OK, then it sounds like it is really up to me, and that you could live with my choice, after I have considered your opinion. Correct?"

Spouse: "Yes." This answer is further clarity. Either the shirt dislike was not strong enough to be an aggravation the rest of the night, or getting to express an opinion was enough input into the decision making to be satisfactory.

You: "Cool." Embrace the conclusion, move on, and smile with satisfaction that a rise in tension eased off in just thirty seconds. Embracing a partner at this moment further seals the interaction in a limbic-soothing way. It is a good excuse—as if an excuse was ever needed—for a juicy hug.

Identify the Emotion

Studies have shown that humans can recognize emotions in a facial expression, even if the image is seen too fast to register in consciousness. High-speed video records the reactions of the study subject's face. The subject flickers a smile if the quickly passing image was smiling, and a frown if the image was frowning. We are hard-wired for emotional awareness and responsiveness.

But our cultural training leads us to suppress our responsiveness. Rejection of emotion blocks motivation to learn about it. Therefore, emotional situations can cause panic.

The littlest bit of information can help. Charles Darwin identified six basic emotions back in 1872: happiness, sadness, anger, fear, disgust, and surprise. This list may not stand the test of scientific time, but it's short and easy to memorize.

When you encounter an emotion, identify which of the six it is. The average person can determine an emotion just by looking at pictures of facial expressions. You may encounter charts that list up to one hundred emotions, and there is validity in that. But most of those are variations or derivatives of the original six. For example, shame could be organized as a subset of fear. The fear of judgment.

If you can identify emotions, your understanding of a situation increases dramatically. You can relax a bit since you don't have to understand or remember all the words. All you need is an appropriate response to the emotion.

Empathetically, smile in the face of happiness and pout in the face of sadness. If a lover reveals a fear, you might say, "That sounds scary." It is not your job to change the emotion or end it. Let it rise, then fall, all on its own.

Focus in on keywords that would indicate fear, frustration, sadness, or any emotion. Repeat to yourself the emotion words you have heard. That brings you closer to feelings, so you project understanding rather than rejection.

At some point in the conversation your lover may cry, or laugh, or identify a feeling. The magical moment has arrived. Your lover has gotten where they needed to go. And you have helped. That feels good. Tune in to the feeling words, as if someone fired a gun, as soon as a feeling word is out there. Try to understand that feeling instead of judging it.

In all situations, empathy is a fail-safe response to emotion. If your lover is happy, let yourself be happy too. Smile, beam, laugh, dance, or cavort. Celebrate the moment. Exercise your happiness muscles. Banish envy and resentment.

What emotion is this lover expressing?

Lover: "I hate my mother!"

The key word is hate. It is an emotional expression word. It is not rational. The emotion is anger. The topic is not your partner's mother, it's your partner's anger, and what might be the hurt underneath the anger. Staying with the salient emotion leads to catharsis, and a return to calm.

Inquiry That Goes Deeper into Feelings

One of you is in a funk, and you want to help, but I recommend never asking what is wrong. That is a judgment.

Nothing is wrong. Your lover is just living. Things happen to people, and they feel things. What could be more ordinary?

If there is no threat to physical safety, then nothing is wrong with any of us. This is a useful, if radical, paradigm. It fundamentally affects the assumptions and expectations that arise in our brains.

"Why did you do that?" is not a good question to ask. It feels like an interrogation.

"How did that feel?" is much better.

Uncovering every single detail you are curious about in what your lover is saying is not useful. That is prioritizing yourself over your lover. Your questions can be sidetracking.

"What color was her hair?" is a question about you. It is something you want to know, but it has no relevance.

"Wow, did you like her hair?" This question is about your lover's experience.

The purpose of inquiry is to understand what emotion your lover is feeling. A side benefit is helping its expression. Your calm presence may be all that is needed. Your lover will know you are there, and if you are giving off a vibe of genuine support, they may feel comfortable enough to share what is going on.

Whatever need you have to know, right now, is a demand made by your ego. Satisfying your curiosity is about you. Inquiry is about your lover. Questions can easily sidetrack the flow. Err on the side of less input. Statements are often the most effective form of inquiry.

"It looks like you were depressed by your friend's story."

Successful inquiry is felt and responded to. You are not the judge. You have to accept your lover's view of it. Good inquiry will energize your lover.

You and your lover were probably not trained to listen and inquire well, so your lover may not be good at it. If you feel that your thoughts and feelings are being blocked, notice that before you get angry, or withdrawn. Point out the blocking words to your partner and speak the words you would like to hear. Repeat until they get it right.

Empathize

Lovers start out in blissful harmony, but over time diverge. An undercurrent of criticism plays out in brains, interfering with total love and acceptance. Understanding, appreciation, and empathy dissipate. The relationship bond weakens.

That can be fixed. Empathy can be reactivated through practice. The ability to turn it on is a superpower. If you have ever been in love, or ever felt empathetic, you can pop into that state at will.

Lives can be overfull with work, obligation, and responsibility. It's nice to have a little escape, like going to a movie. Movies are entertaining, but also inspiring or cathartic. They can stimulate our emotions. Make us feel alive again, for a moment at least.

Drama on the movie screen can evoke empathy. We cringe when a character suffers and beam when they are victorious. Lovers can evoke such empathetic reactions in us if we are not in a habit of reacting negatively.

A negative reaction habit leads to suffering for both partners. Suffering and unease may be the state you are most familiar with. If empathy seems a long was off, a first step, which can be achieved through discipline, is compassion. Compassion can be more sustainable than empathy. Psychological studies have shown that compassion is a more generalized, even detached caring.

But your lover benefits from empathy more than compassion. Chapter 5 describes empathy in more detail, and how to pop into it, safely and unburdened.

Provide Physical Comfort

The fear of making a mistake, or making a situation worse, stops you from moving into closer physical contact when your lover gets emotional. But keeping a physical distance is not comforting, unless requested.

Start with the assumption that physical comfort will be helpful. Approach from the safest angle, if you're concerned. Begin with peripheral locations such as feet, lower legs, hands, forearms, and the back. These locations feel the safest to upset people. Graceful, slow movement closer will signal a comforting intent.

Emotional isolation is painful. Finding an unobtrusive spot to place one hand, and just keeping it there, can be relieving. Physical touch counters unpleasant thoughts, such as, "I'm so alone."

The effect of touch can take time. Perhaps fifteen minutes or more. It might seem like nothing is happening, but it is. Sometimes touch can soothe when words can't. If your touch is allowed, then don't remove it.

Humans have high touch needs, so give comforting or sensual touch to your partner whenever you are together. Over time, your lover will associate your touch with something good. You can collect on that when things get sticky.

Seeing yourself touching tenderly can induce empathy in you. It forces you to overcome your resistance, and a possible habit of isolating your physical self away from an emotional partner. Physical isolation is a way of nonverbally saying,

"That's your shit, and I reject it. I will remain over here, so I can think my critical and judgmental thoughts about you to my heart's content."

Holding a steady touch mellows out your thoughts. That helps you both. Think of yourself as a therapy dog. Dogs are aggressive and defensive, but can shift to behaving empathetically, even under research conditions, as reported in the journal *Animal Cognition*:

"Researchers Custance and Mayer put individual dogs in an enclosure with their owner and a stranger. When the participants were talking or humming, the dog showed no behavioral changes, however, when the participants were pretending to cry, the dogs oriented their behavior toward the person in distress . . . in a submissive fashion, by sniffing, licking and nuzzling the distressed person."

An excellent model for offering comfort. Now just translate that into human behavior. I have, on occasion, pretended to be a dog. Putting my nose in and sniffing, to test the waters of interaction. Such playfulness almost always lowers tension.

Be Supportive and Celebratory

Start with the assumption that your lover is smart, together, successful, sexy, fun, and happy. These qualities are all good, right? They deserve congratulations. Your attention to those aspects of your lover encourages a higher frequency of those stellar aspects. Your approval, acknowledgment, and encouragement are needed more than you realize.

Encouragement is felt on many levels. It is not a rational thing. But the limbic system feels it. A lover's enthusiasm is not a bottomless resource. It can be dimmed by inadequate light. Resistance to giving encouragement is important information to address, instead of ignoring.

Perhaps you are annoyed by certain topics and communication styles. Alas, this irritant will surface after the peak. It's hard to be encouraging when thoughts such as "I wish he would notice that I hate politics," or, "I wish she would drop the idea of a Hawaiian vacation," keep repeating.

It is helpful to separate "state" from "content." In both cases above, a lover's excitement glow can be loved and cherished by focusing first on the state of excitement. Try to get what joy you can from emulating a lover's topical arousal. After that wave has moderated, then you can reveal how the specific content is challenging, if it still is after the fun.

Often, one partner of a dyad is more communicative and expressive than the other, and that is OK, as long as both partners try to stretch in the other's direction.

The more talkative and expressive communication style does not prioritize an efficient transfer of information. It is a blossoming of possibilities and directions, a tapping around inside to find where something is felt.

The more linear or impatient partner may want to jump in, to end it or change it. That is interference. The point of talking is not to elicit analysis. The point is to hear oneself speak. To get thoughts and feelings uploaded to the cosmic hard drive.

Each path through the same material releases more pent-up energy. The desire to intervene is just ego. Attention is all that is needed, along with the occasional sound of support, such as "right," "cool," "I see." So little effort is required, it feels like you're not doing enough. But it is enough.

Relax into knowing you are being as supportive you can be. The required patience takes discipline. You can get bored. You may need to think about something else, while you continue to track the primary topics your partner is exploring, but show interest in each new thing that comes up.

Enthusiasm feels good. Why not let yourself feel it? Perhaps you are not in the mood. Is there something sacred about your mood? There is no easier way of getting out of a funk than being uplifted by your partner. All you have to do is not block the energy coming in your direction.

Every day our partners initiate something. They want to feel alive. We can help them, or stifle them. Over time, how we respond to our partner's "bids" is one of the primary indicators of the success of our relationship. We need our partners to witness us. I can't overstate the importance of it.

If you hear something horrifying, like "I would love to do a threesome with Jamie" (assuming the idea doesn't turn you on), breathe, and try to find the smallest shred of interest. Even if you know in your bones you would never do the something being suggested, give a little time for your partner's expression to complete itself. Then you can reveal what seems impossible for you to overcome, always viewed as a trigger, fear, or limitation you have, instead of a judgment of your lover. Desire is a precious thing. Try not to shame it.

This is everyday Tantra in action. Trying to get more and more out of the smallest things, like the smell of her hair, or the deep rumbling of his voice. Prioritize what keeps you in an appreciative instead of a rejecting state.

What Are You Vulnerable About?

If you are uncomfortable, stiff, awkward, anxious, or selfconscious, something is bothering you. A first step could be to soothe yourself. Remind yourself that you will be OK.

Your attention can remain divided as you contemplate

what is bothering you. Tension from a hard day at work may cause you to snap at little things, like your lover being late to a dinner date.

A long drink of water fails to quench your aggravation. You've had issues with a coworker before and are embarrassed that they persist. You could pretend your anger is only about tardiness. But in reality, you are angry with yourself. Anger toward your lover is misplaced.

If self-soothing hasn't helped, it's time to reveal the discomfort. The more vulnerable you are, the more empathetic your lover will be. Nothing is more natural. Vulnerability means you speak about the emotions you are feeling, such as shame. Nothing more is needed.

Don't expect your partner to fix you or your problem. That would be whining. Whining means you can't accept reality. Emotional maturity is accepting your authentic reality and overcoming any shame you have about it.

A mountain of shame is programmed into all of us. It takes a lot of courage to overcome shame and reveal our truth. People recognize that courage and respect it. There is some risk. If you are with an immature person, you might be judged or laughed at. That moment could hurt, but then you know the character of your company.

As shame recedes, self-confidence increases. You become more of your own sounding board, and less sensitive to the responses you get to your vulnerability. Your vulnerability is a precious gift to the world. It models for us all that humans are not perfect. Many of our historical standards are unnatural and inhuman and isolate us from each other.

If your lover has noticed your distress and asked you about it, that is awesome! They have invited you to share. Do it. You don't earn points by denying there is a problem. Give your partner a chance to help you. Help may simply be both of you witnessing your truth.

That means revealing things that hurt you, not what you are angry about or critical of.

Imagine your lover saying "I'm going out with friends," at the exact moment you felt the need to talk about your day.

An angry/defensive response is: "Really? Your friends are such losers."

The vulnerable emotion is sadness, due to a need that is not met.

Reveal, and hope for the best. "OK babe. Have a good time. I had a bit of a hard day. Can we cuddle when you get back?"

Vulnerability invites understanding, compassion, and empathy. Attacking invites a counterattack, which is the opposite of comfort.

Revealing your tender underbelly reduces the stress of having to maintain a tough exterior and gives your lover permission to do the same. That puts you both on the gentle escalator to relationship peace.

What if you are depressed a lot? Don't people tire of hearing about it? Yes. But you can heighten their interest in your story through the quality of delivery. That may mean not taking yourself so seriously, speaking with some detachment, as if you're in a play. Your story could then show that you are handling your adversity, which could inspire the listener.

Revealing vulnerability is a little moment of therapy, which helps you process something through. You speak, and you notice you didn't die. That is encouraging. There is a tendency to try harder when you are witnessed, versus when you are alone in your head.

The quicker you get to the nugget of what you are feeling, the less patience your partner needs. Offering a time limit, such as five minutes, may help your partner overcome their resistance to listening. When the time is up, be grateful, and accept that the interlude is complete.

Tim Ferriss, author of *The 4-Hour Workweek* and popular podcaster, is a good model of successful vulnerability. He reveals a lot about his mind, emotions, and body during his podcasts. That brings the listener in. An adult lifetime of communicating his limitations, weaknesses, and gaps in knowledge, has led to massive personal and professional growth for him.

If you are overwhelmed by something you are going through, you may need professional help, as a first step. Where and when to be vulnerable may take time to fine-tune. If your lover never empathizes with your vulnerable shares, your only outlet may be friends or therapists, until your lover learns the value of the process.

Apologize and Make Up

Something that you say or do will hurt your lover. But you don't have to feel guilty for long. You can fix it. The first step is an apology.

Argh! You might hate apologizing, or be against it on principle. I understand that there can be a financial and legal risk related to apologies since they are regarded as an admission of error, and therefore subject to liability.

But that is the legal world. Your relationship is the emotional world. Apologizing to your lover is an emotional act. It doesn't incur liability. It is an artifact of the moment, and then it is gone.

Learning to separate the rational (complete analysis of worthiness) from the emotional (the needs of your lover) is the key to apologizing. Your lover feels hurt. You may have no idea why. That doesn't matter.

You are not the judge of what is hurtful or not. No matter how silly or inconsequential you think the cause is. Errors are made in either direction. You might think you caused hurt when you did not. Trust your lover's perspective.

The hurt might have been unintentional. Or unconscious. Perhaps a little of your pain leaked out. You might believe you in no way should be held responsible for your lover's feeling of hurt. That may be true, but taking responsibility soothes the hurt. It is purely practical. Only your ego is in the way. Just do it.

Unintentional or unconscious hurt sometimes has an element of intentionality to it. A mini revenge is acted out. If you don't believe that, you may lack the needed self-awareness.

The claim of "joking" does not excuse you. Having a different sense of humor from your lover is normal. But track the effect of your "jokes." If your partner laughs, it was funny. Otherwise, it was not funny and may have been offensive or hurtful.

Your lover's sensitivities might exasperate you. You don't ease them by doubling down. Doing so reveals your resentment and frustration. And is re-traumatizing. Think of sensitivities as phobias. Gentle, controlled exposure is what helps. Your partner observes your facility with the phobia and absorbs a little confidence.

Signs your lover is hurt: looks deflated, defeated, dejected, disappointed, or sad, right after something you said. Observing these reactions gives you the opportunity to course correct.

Holding an apology in your pocket gives you breathing room to try stuff and not fear blowing it. You will blow it at some point. Make that assumption. That is OK. Your lover will not be miffed for long if you have methods of recovery.

Sometimes the recovery can be quick if you catch it in time. A "let me rephrase that," followed by a more thoughtful statement, might do.

Or "I don't know why I said that."

More expressively: "OMG! Did I say that? What a terrible thing to say! I can't believe I said that! Jeez! Weird!" Expressing the surprise and shock that your partner might have felt hearing it.

It's only an apology if feels like an apology to your partner. For example, "I'm sorry you feel like I criticized you," may not feel like an apology, since it implies that your partner did something, instead of you.

In an actual apology, you take full responsibility. "I'm sorry I criticized you."

An apology is an admission that something could have been done in a less disturbing way. That is pretty much always true.

Give the apology time to sink in. Even say it in different ways. If you wish to speed up the process, you can try to make it up to your partner. You can say, "How can I make it up to you?" The makeup might be hard. The harder it is, the more likely you will remember not to repeat the hurt.

Your lover may not want to forgive you, but you still have options. You can offer something so immense, it would be difficult to refuse. For example: "What if I paid you a million dollars?" The size of the makeup offer is not meant to be literal, but to reveal to your partner that a makeup is possible. After that, the size is negotiable.

If your partner asks for an immense makeup, don't trash it. It may only be a challenge to your ego, such as groveling on the floor while you kiss your partner's feet. Do it right then. If there is a material cost, think about spending the money. It might be worth it.

Apologizing is a good first step, but overcoming broken agreements requires more effort. Once trust is broken, it can take a long time to rebuild. You can't blame your partner for how long it takes. You were the one who screwed up. Trust is not rational. It is felt.

Learn by Trial and Error

You can see that something is up, but don't know what it is. What do you do? You can guess. Guessing is an excellent test of your knowledge. You are the student, and your partner is the teacher. Grading is pass/fail.

Enter the test as relaxed and confident as possible. This gives you access to your most acute observations. Observation is further aided by being as blank, or nonreactive, as possible.

Observation: My partner looks dejected. Is that disappointment, sadness, or physical pain? Remember, it's not a test, if you ask what's "wrong." And nothing is "wrong" anyway. It just is.

Throw out your best guess and see what happens.

You: "Hi honey, it looks like you're disappointed with the cereal you bought yesterday."

Honey: "Bleck! It tastes like cardboard." "Bleck" is cathartic. You helped your partner unload that disappointment.

That was a "hit," or correct guess. A hit is comforting or cathartic and helps move something along. A miss either does nothing or increases agitation.

It is crucial to not get annoyed if you miss. You *cannot* blame your partner. No matter how hard you tried, or how accurate you thought you were, you guessed incorrectly. No big deal. Just take it in as information. Pause and try again.

How can you improve your guesses? Look deeper within yourself. Is your attention absorbed by your own feelings? Or is it echoing your lover's feelings? The echo is what you want.

Your lover's reactions tell you if you are hitting or missing. Did she pull away from you, or look confused? Did he sigh in exasperation, or become silent? Those would be indications that you are off the mark.

Stay calm. Your guess was just wrong. Think again and try again. Most lovers will see you are trying. If you don't get it right this time, you will have many more opportunities.

With each try, you learn something. Remember, it is *entirely* up to your lover whether you have guessed well, or not. It's frustrating when you try and fail, but with practice, you'll get better at it.

If your partner is receptive to helping, ask, "What would you like me to say?" Then say those exact words, in the same tone of voice, scrupulously avoiding any sarcasm. Do not deviate one iota, no matter how much you want to edit. You will be amazed how much your partner likes to hear those exact words. That is a model to follow for future interaction.

There is an infinite pool of possible compassionate, understanding, humorous, or empathetic things to say. I have learned to trust that a gem will come. If I, a shy introvert, can be so facile, then so can you.

It doesn't help if you are running insecurities or criticisms in your head when it is time to be understanding. Replace such thoughts by refocusing on observation. So you can take in the smallest clues from your partner's facial expressions, body language, or words.

Communication that hits the mark feels delicious to you both. It is worth putting in the effort. Every small step that improves interactions with your lover makes relationship life easier and more satisfying. Every step makes you more human, and less grizzly.

This chapter detailed techniques for handling a lover's bear. Living and practicing those techniques is useful for oneself, even if a calming effect on a lover is slow in coming. It's relaxing to model relaxed behavior.

The more relaxed you are, the more it is possible to share thoughts and feelings vulnerably instead of angrily. This is the direction of intimacy for you and your lover. And the direction of cuddliness and sex.

It is certainly possible to channel anger into hot sex, but that takes skill. It's also possible for bodies to become aroused in spite of suppressed animosity and a load of unresolved issues.

But as the divide between arousal and intimacy widens, a detached, or resistant arousal works less and less. There is no permanent escape from staying in sync with your partner.

Taming the bear moves you both towards connection, love, sex, and magic.

5

The Magical Power of Empathy

Do you ever get choked up during a movie? If you hear Bonnie Raitt sing "I can't make you love me, if you don't," do you feel a little heartache? If you get the slightest twinge of any feeling, via input from the world outside of your own head, then you were empathetic in that moment. Congratulations! You are human.

It is possible to feel an emotion at any time on any day. The evocative source could be music, a movie, or a lover's story. When dopamine tapers off, those feelings may be different than when you started out together. Happiness could be less common, and anger more noticeable.

It might even seem like emotions of all types have mysteriously diminished. That trend can be reversed. Feeling emotionally alive, even with a long-term partner, is always possible, although some practice is required.

A practice of opening to more emotional aliveness, in all aspects of life, can be harnessed for use in relationships by seeding empathy. The practice of empathy toward people in general can leak over toward your partner. Such an effect can happen even if you are resistant.

Passion is squashed by repeating angry thoughts about our partners over and over again in our heads. Thought improvement can be approached sideways. If your heart has hardened toward your partner, a different person or event can make you tear up.

If you don't fight it, it feels good. The act of caring for another person feels good. It is a gift to yourself. On the verge of conflict, empathy can take an interaction in a happier direction. Empathy has the power to unstick the most sticky situation.

An agitated bear (lover) is seldom soothed by rational discussion, because the source of agitation is not rational. It is emotional. I like rational thinking as much as anyone, but we don't always have a choice. Every day, we find ourselves in moments that are spontaneous and emotional. Once that happens, as soon as the moment tips emotional, it is most efficient to flow *with* emotions, instead of fighting them. Empathy encourages that flow. Emotions get released, and all is good.

Five seconds of empathy can be more valuable to your lover than five hours of discussion, or any rational interaction. That is because empathy is felt, and has an effect. Jabbering is a way to maintain distance. To avoid feeling.

Joining in with another person's emotions is empathy. Feeling the *same* emotions as another person, at the same time. I have learned to embrace such moments as deliciously alive.

One can choose to be empathetic. It works even if the motivation is a desire to feel better, or not stay stuck. When a lover feels empathy, they bathe in love. There is nothing better you can give. And it doesn't cost a penny.

Here is a brief script that helps to define empathy:

A text comes in to your phone. "Call me right away."

You call and hear crying. "Last night . . . I had a serious accident."

"Oh no!" **That's empathy.** "Really?" Not empathy.

"In the middle of the night . . . I got up to pee. On the way back . . . I fell down the stairs."

The shocked inrush of air. **Empathetic.** "Uh-huh." Not empathetic.

"I could have died, and you were not there to help me."

"Oh, babe! That sounds terrible! I don't want you to die!" **Yep, empathetic.** "But you knew I had this trip planned for months." Defensive instead of empathetic.

Five seconds of empathy transfers an ocean of love. That is what's needed. That is what heals an aching heart and eases physical pain. Detached observation, or defense of any kind, further injures the heart. We crave love that much. By a lucky coincidence, giving empathy feels better than giving any other response. The state of empathy is its own reward.

Reward and Risk

Evolution has given humans a reward for feeling empathetic, so it has survival value. Empathy gives us a window into our fellow humans, to better understand the world we find ourselves in. Empathy probably evolved as a side effect of "mirror" neurons that facilitate the instant learning of physical movements. We see a dance move, and can visualize it, or perform the same movements.

Our brains copy the movements we see. The same is true with facial expressions, and emotions. Before you can stop it, an emotion is copied into your brain, and you feel that emotion too. Genetic factors, related to autism, can reduce or eliminate this ability.

A scary term for the ease of copying is "emotional contagion." You don't mind the contagion while watching your favorite sports team crush an opponent. But you resist the contagion, and resent its infiltration, if your lover is unhappy. The contagion challenges your sense of autonomy.

Resisting emotional contagion, or a lover in need of emotional support, stimulates our discomfort wiring. It's a battle between altruism and autonomy. As time passes, those competing impulses escalate. Body, mind, and spirit are weakened. Then it gets worse.

Partner: "Do you still love me?"

Uncomfortable sensations flood the body, and override rational thinking. You assign your lover responsibility for the pain you feel. But that is inaccurate. Negative responses were implanted in your body over the course of a lifetime, waiting for activation.

Imagine you are diabetic. Your pancreas produces less insulin than needed to process sugar. But sometimes you eat a whole bag of cookies, then feel sick. You feel so crappy that you chop up the bag with an ax and destroy your kitchen floor. You blamed the cookies, but the real culprit was your diabetes.

Your lover's words, or emotions, like sugar, can cause physical distress. A spike in emotional output can be nauseating, and panicking, like a spike in blood sugar. We want to destroy the "cookies," and our lover for providing them. We are as clueless as an undiagnosed diabetic.

A Distress Reaction

Becoming fearful and distressed from the distress of others is the average behavior of infants under two years of age. Older children exhibit empathy. They understand that the emotions of another child are that child's emotions, and can shift to helping.

A few years further in development, empathy is overridden by dominance pursuits, which stay in place until hormones stimulate interest in sexuality, which young people are untrained for.

The result is what we see, lots of sexual and emotional interactions that end up painful for one or both participants. The lack of emotional skills leads to distress in the form of confusion, hurt, and anger.

Our inner babies are ever ready to squall. My blood boils when Cheryl is hesitant about an interest, desire, or plan of mine. Sometimes I can laugh at my infantile reactions. Or breathe through them and remember that underneath my rage is rejection. Once I reveal my defeated sadness, Cheryl becomes more sympathetic.

If I try to suppress feelings of rejection, muscles tighten up in my jaw, and my throat gets dry. My body signals distress. It lets me know something is up so I can deal with it, instead of getting angry or freezing up.

Choking up is another signal that could be interpreted as distress, but more accurately as the beginning stage of an emotion such as sadness or gratitude.

In my experience, choking up, and other physical discomforts, are not caused by the emotion itself, but by resistance to expressing the emotion. Crying with sadness is the release, or relief of, the sadness.

A Fluid Reaction

If one is emotionally "fluid," emotions just come and go, leaving no memory in the mind, or body. Discomfort is in the resistance, like heat in an electrical fuse. A fuse limits the flow of electricity. If that limit is surpassed, the fuse heats up and melts. The circuit breaks. If your emotional circuit overloads, your discomfort fuse maxes out, and you lash out.

Gaining greater comfort with emotions is like growing bigger circuits, and fuses, so you can handle your lover's spikes in emotional energy. You can join in and not be afraid.

If you don't fear emotional contagion, you don't have to fight it when it happens. You can just let it flow through you, laughing, or crying, with the understanding you are channeling, not originating these expressions. The only meaning in the moment is that you are being emotionally fluid.

Fear of contagion is reduced if you separate expressions of emotion from commitments and actions. In the empathetic moment, don't commit to anything. In most cases, your empathy is all that is needed. Most people are not looking to take advantage of you. They are grateful enough that you are empathetic.

Your empathetic experience can remain within your own body, separate from your lover's. When you have an alcoholic drink, you know you're going on a ride. You don't think of yourself as the alcohol. The alcohol is just doing something to you. It means nothing. If you are not thinking of the dangers of drink, you can enjoy a couple. In the same way, you can enjoy the emotional ride your lover takes you on.

There are over a hundred subtle emotions beyond the primary six. They can be viewed as different drink categories, like beer compared to tequila. Quality can vary within categories, but the more expert the drinker, the more all categories are appreciated. The more emotionally fluid you are, the less emotion categories are felt as "good" or "bad."

Changing the good/bad dynamic gives you more slack for your lover's emotions and, crucially, for your reactions. It helps you distinguish the difference. You can say to yourself, "Honey is sad, and that brings up fear for me. I need to drop my fear so I can be sad too. That keeps us in sync."

Empathy is feeling your *lover's* emotions, instead of your own. Your identity can be unaffected. They are your lover's emotions, not yours. That is how you maintain your sense of safety. You remain autonomous. No matter how pitiful a lover's feelings might seem, you don't have to fix them. Just feel them.

Flying off with your own reactions is the opposite of empathy.

Dismissing a Danger

Some people believe that "energy," in the form of thoughts and feelings, travels through the air, passes through the skin, and inhabits the body of another. But that would violate the laws of physics, since no waves in the electromagnetic spectrum can directly transport brain activity outside the brain. It is only fear-inducing to take on such beliefs.

Neural networks create emotions in our brains. Like blood flowing through arteries, emotions are discretely contained within bodies. Your only exposure to the emotions of others is through sounds or sights.

Sound waves travel, enter your ears, and are processed by your brain. Facial expressions emit light waves that enter your eyes. If there is no physical contact, a lover's emotional expression has no more impact on you than watching a movie.

But few of us are trained as emotional wave surfers. We quiver in fear if an emotional tsunami is bearing down on us. We act out in ways we don't expect. Our family and re-lationship history has built in sensitivity to many types of emotional floods.

We nearly black out when these sensitivities are acti-vated. The trick is how quickly can one diagnose and treat sensitivity reactions before they are externalized as blame.

Distress and discomfort reduce easy-flowing social abili-ties, so a habit of switching from fear to empathy, is very use-ful. Flip that switch when you're uncertain how to behave. It's like waving a magic wand or changing into a superhero costume. It gives you the ability to surf back to the beach, and re-connect to present time.

If a friend's child has died, for example, and you attend the funeral, you may be uncertain how to behave toward your friend. But if you can switch to empathy, you can let in the grief of loss. Feeling grief is the most appropriate re-sponse. Joining with the parents, and community, to feel grief eliminates discomfort, and helps with the needed heal-ing. The more grief, the better. I would say the child's death is not honored if it is not grieved, as many or our ancestors believed.

Empathy clears up confusion. Move close and cry too. Your family, community, or lover will feel you, and won't have to deal with your discomfort. If you are not resistant, or afraid of emotional contagion, the experience can at least be painless. And potentially blissful.

Resistance

Your lover wants you to get high (excited), happy, or even sad with them. You may resent giving a lover power over our emotional state. I used to be firmly in that camp. But then I realized that my mood was not that special.

In a moment of resistance to your lover, ask yourself this question: "Is my mood sacred?"

The degree that you resist your lover's emotional state is the degree that you clamp down on your own emotional fluidity. A habit of suppressing a lover's feelings becomes generalized, resulting is self suppression.

You might be thinking, "I should feel happy, sad, or depressed, along with my partner? That seems so weird. If I get depressed too, then we both just go down."

Good point. Empathetic responses vary, depending on the emotion. Dropping into sadness, or gratitude, with your lover feels good. There is plenty to be sad or grateful about. Your lover gives you a chance to express it. Depression is a state of powerlessness over a *lack* of emotional expression. An empathetic support would not to be depressed too, but to help your lover feel the grief, fear, anger, or shame that is locked down.

Empathetic, or Not?

Learning what an empathetic response is takes practice. It can be tricky. An addled brain can override judgment. Empathy is *not* expressing your own reactions to someone else's expressions. If your lover is getting further agitated, then you are not being empathetic, no matter what you think.

You are being empathetic *if it feels empathetic to your lover.*

Empathy is taking a step beyond ego pause. It's dissolving the boundary between you and your lover. Stepping from observer to participant. Dissolving the boundary is intimate, and that can be scary.

Can the boundary of "self" dissolve? The chemical DMT, an active ingredient in ayahuasca, the traditional spiritual medicine of the Amazon, can create a terrifying experience of complete body dissolution. A milder, blissful version of dissolution is achieved through meditation, which stimulates natural DMT production in the pineal gland of our brains.

Self softening, through meditation, correlates with a sense of oneness with the universe. Oneness pleasure is also a side effect of intimacy with a lover. A relaxing of individual identity facilitates emotional openness and makes interacting with a lover a transcendental experience.

Replacing rigidity with empathy allows the dividing lines between thoughts, feelings, sensations, and mystical experience to fade away. Along with judgment and criticism, of self and other. Such a peak of empathy may be even better than being in love since lovers can chose to activate it. Magic is a choice.

Speed to Empathy

How fast you can pop into empathy is a factor in successful outcomes. Your lover wants your love (or empathy) instantly, and notices if you are not giving it instantly. The more you resist giving empathy, the more rejected your lover may feel. The more rejected your lover feels, the more empathy is required.

On and on it goes until a blowup ensues, which could take hours, days, or weeks to patch up. As you know, that is a *lot* of effort.

By comparison, empathy is effortless. Switch to empathy and enjoy a moment of connection with your partner. Or resist, and put out a thousand times the effort to correct your resistance. Do you want to be practical or stubborn?

There is also a correlation between depth of empathy (quality) and whether empathy is felt, or not. Habits of resistance stand in the way of quality.

Magical Examples

Here is an example from real life that illustrates the magical power of empathy:

Male lover: "I hate you!"

Female lover: "Of course! I hate myself! In fact, I can't stand myself!"

An outside observer might take offense and think, "How can she say that about herself?" But because she was fluid, she rode the energy coming at her and transformed it. It just came and went. Her ability to merge with the attack on her deflected the emotional charge and left the man holding the pressure of what he started.

The pressure fizzled as both partners cracked up laughing. And the male lover amended his outburst by saying, "No, I don't really hate you. No one should hate you." He ended up defending his partner. A complete reversal.

How differently the scene would have played out if her response had been "I hate you too!"

The empathetic lover gains power, and control over the moment, by flowing with the energy, instead of firing back. Like aikido, this focuses the attention on the aggressive one, revealing the limit of their abilities. The degree of our outward projection of emotion onto another person equals the degree to which we lack emotional intelligence.

Example two: One day, I was enjoying a conversation during a break from a course in bodywork and healing at a school in Phoenix, Arizona, when a loud voice intruded from the reception area. It persisted, so I investigated. A man was pacing, and yelling, his intent unclear. He had entered the reception area from a busy street.

The belligerent guy was large, young, well-muscled, and drunk. I glanced at the receptionist, who was frozen in panic. Without thinking, I walked up to the young man, smiled, said hello, and embraced him solidly. My head only came up to his shoulder. I beamed love into his heart while I hugged.

If he had wanted, the man could have slammed me onto the floor and beat me senseless. But my actions were so opposite of threatening that he was confused. At that moment, he became malleable.

I hoped that whatever action I took would silence him. Check. Next I told him I wanted to hear his story, and that the best place for that would be outside on a bench. I had to embody sincerity, or he would not have budged. Out we went. We talked for ten minutes. Then he grew silent, and left.

An irony is that to be empathetic you have to let go of your agenda, which will probably lead to accomplishing your agenda. Crazy!

The whole scene, from start to finish, took fifteen minutes of my life. But when the scene ended, it was over, and I seamlessly returned to class. No agitation continued to swirl within my body that would take hours to process and dissipate.

A much longer scene, acted out through confrontation, escalation, and perhaps police involvement, would have filled my body with an overdose of stress hormones. I am not a friend of stress. For me, choosing empathy is a no-brainer.

Empathy Soothing and Pleasure

If I am "empathy real," there is nothing to fear and nothing to fix. It is a moment of limitless possibilities. This is one reason I classify conscious relating as a spiritual path. It takes an element of faith in the methodology, but I have seen it work a high percentage of the time.

Your inner landscape changes when you give empathy, and something even more dramatic happens to the person who receives it. They get as much as or more than they need. They reach completion with the issue at hand .

I used to be overwhelmed by every type of tense situation and wanted to escape them all. But one day I realized that no amount of withdrawal solved the problem. Withdrawing from the field means you close off input on the course of your life. Such opportunities might not return.

By definition, if I am empathetic, I am not in opposition to my lover's thoughts and feelings. I am accepting, and not defensive. It's counterintuitive, but an empathetic attitude makes your negotiating position stronger. Your lover is more able to describe the stress your position causes. Speaking the stress eases it, and opens up the possibility of hearing about your needs.

The transition from tense to disarmed is so relieving, both parties feel a bit giddy. That could result in hugs or sex. The more empathetic you are, the more you can feel when a lover is in the mood. The better mood reader you are, the more confidence and trust your lover puts in you. That trust is a foundation upon which the freest sexual expression can be built.

When a lover's mildest pleasure begins, empathy for that pleasure (feeling your lover's pleasure as your own) is perceived as support, encouraging more pleasure. Cycles of pleasure supporting pleasure keep repeating, with increasing intensity, until a wave of orgasm erupts. And that is just a pause.

Sexual interludes don't always flow seamlessly. An infinite number of interruptions can arise, from getting out condoms and lube, to handling direction about touch locations. The practice of empathy allows lovers to stay with the happiness of the moment, instead of veering off into insecurity, criticism, or fear.

Loving, sensual touch, whenever the opportunity presents itself, keeps lovers' bodies in a subconscious state of positive regard, and sexual openness, that increases the chances of a productive intimate negotiation, instead of crashing back to failure and disappointment.

A sweet or impishly lustful touch can also be therapeutic. I am constantly amazed how touch can bring me out of a crappy, low-blood-sugar state, either as the giver or the receiver. The concept is stupidly simple: Focus attention on something better. Something better then replaces pain awareness throughout your nervous system.

Pain is malleable. The placebo effect proves it. Mood is

even more malleable and receptive to input. Your partner is annoyed. You empathize. Poof, annoyance gone. The smaller the upset, the quicker empathy soothes it.

Since we are wired for empathy, it is natural to care about a lover. But we don't always care. In those moments, we can ask ourselves why. There is always a reason for resistance to caring (empathy). When you feel that resistance, you can connect the dots of its cause, which at least opens up the possibility of addressing the deeper problem.

Resistance to empathy for your partner is not a fatal flaw. But it is an important indicator that something is up. That something is significant. It is affecting all of your interactions. Something is not working for you, so you need to address it, or let it go.

When you accept responsibility for resistance to your partner, you can just decide to be empathetic. Imagine you have dropped Ecstasy, just got out of a yoga class, or are sipping Lulu's drinking chocolate. Empathy is a good mood, by definition. That can motivate you.

According to a recent theory of emotions, in *How Emotions Are Made: The Secret Life of the Brain*, by Professor Lisa Feldman Barrett, emotions are names we give to body sensations. Our culture trains us to give those sensations meaning; therefore the meaning is flexible. We can recreate meanings based on our own experiences.

As a young person, I struggled with insecurity and depression. Discovering yoga made a huge difference for me. After ninety minutes of class, all was right with my world. It was empowering to know I could use my body to reduce my negative thoughts and open my heart.

Not just yoga, but hundreds of activities can have this effect, from Thai Chi to tanning. You can partake in an activity that improves your mood, and if you let it, your attitude toward your partner. Attitude is crucial, and attitude is changeable.

If you can change your attitude through physical activity, then you can learn to change it at will, giving you unprecedented control over your life, and relationships.

Motivations to Be Empathetic

I know how hard it can be to dredge up empathy for a partner when a situation is tense. Escaping in any way possible is the urge. But here are some ways to look at empathy that make it a better option than fleeing the scene.

- Empathy feels good.
- Empathy feels better than habits of fear and anxiety.
- Empathy improves sex.
- It's a cure for self-consciousness
- And a surefire way to handle emotional situations.
- Empathy improves negotiations.
- Resistance to empathy reveals a lot about *yourself.*
- Empathy makes you more functional under duress.
- Empathy increases your knowledge of emotions.
- And increases your knowledge of your lover.
- Empathy opens up limitless possibilities.

If these reasons sound good to you, and you would like to learn more about developing your natural empathetic abilities, you will find practical methods in Chapter 7.

6

The Trouble with Triggers

Love, compassion, and empathy feel fantastic. And it is possible to flip into those states at will, most of the time. But occasionally, we are too annoyed, angry, disappointed, frustrated, or disgusted with a lover to care about their feelings. We are trapped in our own pain and cannot get out. This is the state of being triggered.

You may have heard the phrase "push your buttons." Someone has pushed your buttons if you have an uncontrollable reaction to something that person says or does, such as flushed cheeks, stunned silence, clenched jaws, a spike in blood pressure, or a verbal outburst.

"Triggered" is another way of saying your buttons have been pushed. In the context of lovers, it is assumed to happen accidentally, by lovers just being themselves.

A trigger is a current reaction based on a stressful experience from the past, which gets reactivated. When we are triggered, it seems like a moment of unique clarity or ample justification for a hot-tempered reaction. We feel righteous and angrily blame our lovers for the disturbance.

Almost anything can be triggering, including smells and tastes. A trigger is any input that throws you "off," that short-circuits your normal functioning.

Imagine you are having drinks at a bar, and a friend excitedly exclaims: "I've made a killing on Bitcoin this year." You try to smile, but inwardly you collapse since your own investment account lost big. It feels like a knife stabbing you in the gut. Your friend reminded you of your recent financial pain. Your friend "triggered" the pain.

In reality, that pain could be triggered by many sources, such as a Marketplace report on NPR. Inadequacy regarding money is a common trigger. So is sexual shame, rejection, and jealousy. If physical abuse is involved, then the triggers are buried incomprehensibly deep.

All of us have uncontrollable reactions poised for activation, and someone, or something, will activate them. It's like pulling the trigger of a gun, which is almost comical to think about. We are all carrying around guns pointed at ourselves. We know about them, intuitively, and unconsciously try to avoid situations where those guns will fire.

The guns and triggers were planted inside us by traumatic experiences in our lives when our sensitivities met their worst enemies. Abusive family members, religions, and sexual partners are common sources.

I became introverted and self-conscious as I entered adolescence and was rewarded with increased pressure from my peers to stand up for myself. I failed, compared to the most popular guys, who dated the most popular girls. To this day, I carry some of that trauma and can get a defeated feeling when I see a woman I'm attracted to. I have not completely healed from my earlier powerlessness. My body knows it.

A jealousy trigger might have parental abandonment at its base. A controlling trigger might be rebellion against autocratic parents. The inability to listen to a specific piece of music could be related to a relationship breakup.

Everyone has something that can act as a trigger. Therefore, it will happen to you. You will feel terrible. You wish it hadn't happened and may blame your lover for the pain you feel. Or you might suppress your discomfort, to cover an exposed weakness.

It also feels terrible to see your lover triggered. This happens even at moments when you are happy, excited, or sharing something intimate. If your lover gets triggered by that, it can be very disappointing or annoying.

We have a sixth sense about triggers. Intuition tells us that a triggering situation is near, or upon us. Panic rises, along with tingling at the back of the neck, or a fluttering in the belly. Adrenaline flows into the bloodstream in preparation for fight or flight.

The subconscious mind interprets such arousal signals as a threat. It senses that control over unexpressed emotions is being lost. Those emotions seek a way to come out.

Some Symptoms of Emotional Triggering

- A reflex reaction (rapid escalation)
- An automatic reaction (beyond your control)
- Confusing intensity (does not match situation)
- Abnormal physical sensations (feel weird)
- Intense feelings persist (can't shake them)

Like laughter, triggering just strikes.

A big smile spreads across your lover's face. "Let's talk about my birthday plans!"

You try to smile, but the blood drains from your face. Memories of an abusive relationship are vividly recalled. Your mind screams, "Nooooooo!"

A former lover expected birthday perfection, and you could never live up to it. Ideally, your current lover would never mention birthdays as long as you live. It hurts that much. You have shot yourself.

Your current lover is not to blame for your birthday trigger. The fundamental truth is: No lover is to blame. If the abuse occurred before the two of you met, that truth is obvious. But triggers are not rational.

If you had had the skills you needed earlier in life, you would have handled birthday performance pressure, no matter how bad, and that trigger would not exist.

But triggers are part of every lover package. One could search the planet for a partner that is the least likely to trigger you, *and* the least likely to be triggered *by* you. The cost of such a search would be prohibitive for most people, and the result would not eliminate all risk. We try to have control over our choices, but most likely we just fall in love, which renders us blind to triggers anyway.

When the blinders come off, our partner's triggers shock us. And we dread the effect *our* triggers might have. Being in trigger is embarrassing. We would all choose not to be triggered if we could. Understanding that gives us an opening to view triggers empathetically. If there is any blame to assign, it is to our culture, or life in general. In the current state of human affairs, it is impossible not to collect triggers. And none of us are trained to handle them.

It's not always obvious. If your lover gets angry at you for leaving your toothpaste tube on the sink overnight, you may wonder why it's such a big deal. But your lover feels justified. Your lover's parents enforced rigorous organizational standards, and your lover has internalized them. Your partner can't control those reactions because of unreleased anger from the parents' harsh treatment.

Harshness is normal behavior to your lover. There are no steps between observing the toothpaste and getting angry. The fewer the steps, the more suppressed the underlying emotion.

Freezing is another trigger response, rendering us inoperative like Star Wars robot, C3PO, in recharge mode. Unlike C3PO, however, we are still acutely aware of pain, like a torture drug that immobilizes muscles, yet enhances sensations. We see our lover as the torturer.

Studies on torture have revealed that people will say or do anything to stop the pain. They snap. They act in ways they can't recognize as themselves. The intensity of relationship can create a similar amount of snapping pressure. Like Chinese water torture, found to be effective by *MythBusters*, something has to change or you will go insane.

Fight, Flight, or Freeze

Attacking a lover is a release from the pain and pressure. It is one of three responses to threats: fight, flight, and freeze. By definition, you will respond in one of these ways if you are triggered.

Fighting reinforces the trigger because it adds fresh emotional wounding to an existing issue.

Flight also reinforces the trigger, by taking away partner support that could help modulate a cascade of negative thoughts.

Freezing can feel powerless, but is the most useful response. It focuses the pain of triggering within, where it originates. It's the only response that lets in the hope of progress, since there is the possibility of feeling better after at least talking about it.

Your trigger activates, then you notice the urge toward fight, flight, or freeze. Noticing the urge is a key first step. Increased self awareness gives you a chance to delay implementing your urge. A chance to search for what vulnerable emotion might be in need of expression.

For example, when rage flashes, and my body and brain freeze in reaction to Cheryl's resistance, the underlying emotion is sadness. If I let myself, I would cry over the "perceived" loss of a dream. This trigger is buried in my unprocessed past. A legacy of mismatch with my parents.

If you are in a safe place or can get to a safe place, expressing emotion is ideal. A safe place means an environment, with or without people, where you are not in danger if you expose your vulnerability. In such a space you can take ownership of your process, instead of using your trigger as the perfect opportunity to dump on your lover.

Most of us are familiar with fleeing or fighting. We assume those are standard actions to take under the circumstances. We take those actions because the pain of freezing is too awful. Freezing is like being sick. There is a sense of defeat, emptiness, and nausea, without relief. We want to end it.

I propose bearing the pain of freezing. Masochistic, perhaps, but worth it. Use discipline to endure the pain for an entire day, evening, or night, with hope that something changes for the better.

Not the End of the World

No matter how bad a trigger makes me feel, I know it is only temporary. I can survive it and feel better.

You know what getting sick from bad food is like. Waves of dizziness and nausea begin, which worsen over time, and finally erupt in puke and poo. After that eruption comes relief. Freezing is like the initial phase of sickness, and though it doesn't get to the puking relief stage, it is a bearable level of discomfort.

And you don't have to bear it alone. Your partner will see that something is bothering you. You can reveal that you are triggered. It is not essential to know what the trigger is, just as you might not know which food made you sick.

Assess the level of safety you feel with your partner. You are responsible for your triggers, so determine the best combination of working on them by yourself and with your partner.

Accept your triggers; don't think of them as something to avoid. The more you allow yourself to feel them, the more you will learn about them. As with phobias, progress is made through controlled exposure.

If you are afraid of roller coasters, for example, you could study the history and stats of accidents. Perhaps watch some roller-coaster videos. A bearable level of exposure reduces the irrational component.

A Lover's Trigger

It is tough to understand the irrational aspects of our partners. We want those aspects gone. What can we do? A partner's trauma is something they have to work on. Being relaxed and non-judgmental at least gives safety for processing. Attempting to help with the aftereffects of childhood abuse is very risky. That takes specialized training. It is super-easy to make a mistake that leads to more hurt, instead of healing.

It might be hard to believe, but a triggered lover wants to be with you at that moment. Suppressed emotions have been suppressed for good reason. Those emotions were rejected before. Your fleeing or fighting reinforces that rejection.

Imagine your lover carries shame about crooked teeth, and tries to keep from smiling. You notice this and inquire. Reluctantly, your partner reveals the offending teeth, and you recoil in disgust. The word "trash" appears in your brain. You can't think of anything nice to say.

This is a painful moment for you. However, it's a hundred times worse for your lover, who feels like life is ending. Your partner's worst fear, that all potential lovers will reject them, is coming true.

Each partner is 100 percent responsible for their own emotions. But when triggers arise, try to be compassionate, or empathetic, instead of criticizing, blaming, or rejecting. Avoid wielding non-responsibility as a weapon. As a way to punish your partner.

If you are compassionate enough, you can offer space for emotional expression. Feeling and expressing those emotions may help your lover understand the connection between trigger reactions and the underlying trauma.

You may be accused of causing of the trigger. Your lover might be angry with you. It is hard not to take it personally in these moments, but try not to. You can't escape hurting your lover. Something you say or do, just being yourself, will hurt. How can you not be yourself? It doesn't seem fair.

It isn't fair to be blamed for your partner's trigger. But it happens all the time. If you can stand it, blame and anger can lead to a release for your lover. Hopefully, you can hang in there for the hurt to surface. For the vulnerable part to come out. That only happens if your lover feels safe enough.

The "proximate upset," such as toothpaste on the sink, is not the "real upset." Understanding this can allow you to not take it so personally. The calmer, and more functional, you are under attack, the more likely it is you can lead a partner into self-understanding.

Repeat this thought: "My lover is triggered."

Ignore fairness at this moment. Try not to invalidate the blame coming in your direction. Let the unfairness and irrationality be.

Use all the skills described so far in this book to remain calm and soothing. Keep waiting for the smallest of skills to emerge out of you, for the thinnest crack of an opening back to connection with your lover.

When a lover gets triggered, it is like finding yourself stuck in an underground cave, where a faraway flash flood has cut off the entrance you came in through. It is now pitch-dark, you have no headlamp, the water is rising, and your lover is scared shitless. You must find another exit, but the search is excruciatingly slow, to avoid hitting your heads on rocks, or falling down slippery slopes. If you remain calm, your senses become heightened to the slightest light, or breeze, that might indicate a way out.

Waves of overwhelm crash on your head, and you may wish you were dead. But you don't give up and eventually emerge at the surface. Your feat of survival feels fantastic.

Being stuck in the cave (trigger) was agony, but you did not leave your lover to die.

When you hang in there through the anguish, you both get to witness the return to life. That relief can be so dramatic that hot sex naturally follows.

Being in a trigger is awful, but it is not the complete picture of your relationship. It is just a sliver. You may both be tender for the next few days, but you got through it, learned something about each other, and are closer. If you are open to it, the trigger crucible can change something in you. It can be a step toward reducing the fight-or-flight urgency.

A lover's trigger that frequently repeats is a test of patience. It's hard not to get annoyed if your girlfriend scowls every time you look at a cute waitress. It's hard not to get exasperated when your boyfriend sinks every time he sees his paycheck.

"Get over it already!" you might say. It seems like such an easy thing to do. But it is not. The problem is, anger doesn't help heal the trigger. Only compassion and empathy can do that. Compassion can be hard to dredge up. Discipline may be required, since your lover does not yet have any control over the trigger.

Adopt a neutral attitude that is not encouraging of triggered behavior, yet not critical. Model a different, non-triggered way of being. Try to strike a balance between being yourself and not being controlled by your partner's triggers.

It is a balance or negotiation between absolute freedom and absolute acquiescence. Between the individual authentic self and the self in relationship. Recognize that the relationship self is equally valid. The unaffected authentic self does not exist in relationship.

It Can Be Tricky

As soon as you become lovers, an interplay has begun, which you are not in control of. And if you were, that would be boring, since everyone's imagination is limited in some way.

Your lover adds richness to your life and some tension. The first reaction to tension is the urge to escape. Suppressing that feeling can lead you to resent yourself, but that is not helpful. One can acknowledge motives, and then tweak them, no matter how primitive and self-centered they are.

Imagine that your partner is gleeful about getting a raise. But you can't get excited since it stimulates depressing thoughts about your own career path. Your depression could productively motivate you to do better work, or ask for a raise.

But it is equally possible that you have the urge to do something indulgent, like go to a bar for a drink, or watch the latest episode of *Game of Thrones*, instead of fix dinner. A hidden motivation, the need to escape discomfort, is activated.

The escape motivation is primitive, or base. If spoken, it would reveal painful envy: "Honey, at this moment I hate you for being more successful than me. I don't want to show you how much I hate you, so I am going to get drunk instead."

Often, our partners will notice that something is wrong, and try to find out what it is. And we respond to their questioning with great agitation. The only way out is revealing the truth. I believe the most base motivation is the truest. The motivation that you don't want to admit to yourself, or anyone else. Try to let that in when examining your behavior, and that of others.

The search for the most base motivation can be entertaining. It is a recognition of our humanness and a reminder that we are not "perfect." Hate might be at the first level of awareness, but that is the knee-jerk trigger talking. Underneath that is a crushing weight of self-criticism. If the pain of self-examination is held on to, instead of deflected, a renewed motivation for career progress may result.

How much you can accept your base motivations depends on your degree of shame. The less shame, the more self-acceptance. I am not advocating giving yourself a pass on all your behavior. I'm just saying that as shame reduces, you are more able to see and reveal your real motivations. That is liberating and offers a way to make changes.

If you have examined yourself, and rid yourself of triggering shame, you can confidently and calmly communicate when your partner challenges your motivations or behavior. Buttons can't be pushed if there are no buttons. If you have overcome career performance shame, even the ego stab of a partner's judgment won't mess up your mind.

Since you are reading this book, you may be the most informed partner in the relationship. Your partner may not be aware of the trigger concept, and may only blame, or externalize trigger pain. Your partner may think their behavior is normal, never realizing that their trauma is running things.

Introduce the trigger concept during a calm moment. And hope for the best. When a trigger flares up, let it do its thing, without interference. This is one way to force a partner into self-reflection. Your lack of response highlights the irrationality of trigger behaviors.

When your partner calms down, you can reveal how you feel.

"I feel shamed by your anger. I don't understand it. Is it possible to make a request, instead of getting angry?"

Some anger is justified, for example over a broken agreement. If you broke the agreement, your partner's anger might push you into feeling guilt. Good. That is what guilt is for. Guilt can motivate you to do better.

Nobody is perfect, negotiations are not perfect, and agreements are not perfect, so partners are destined to get triggered, sooner or later. All you can hope for is to handle it gracefully when it happens. Fortunately, well-handled triggers become smaller over time.

Time and patience are what it takes. Patience can be severely tested when a lover goes into trigger. It is common to be triggered by a lover's trigger. Argh.

And You Can Get Lucky

One day, as Cheryl and I were driving through the spectacular landscape of Southern Utah, Cheryl returned to a powerful trigger that had been tormenting her for a couple of years. It involved aggressive criticism by a friend of ours.

I thought Cheryl was over it, but there it was again. I was sick of this trigger and felt like being callously critical. Not a drop of compassion or empathy flowed through my bloodstream. We continued driving along, feeling terrible, for many minutes, unable to appreciate the beauty of the surroundings.

As the silence stretched, the weight of anxiety got too heavy. I had to relieve it. I took a few breaths and turned my mind back to compassion. I replayed in my mind a painful moment with this friend, while we were standing in our kitchen.

A second after visualizing a distraught Cheryl, words popped out of my mouth: "You wish I would have picked her up by the scruff of her neck and tossed her out the front door!"

"Yes!!!!!"

Then we both laughed. That worked. Before the "scruff" statement, we both felt horrible. Afterward, we felt great. I wouldn't have literally thrown a person out of my house, but saying it helped Cheryl feel that I understood her pain.

That moment was a crystallization of concepts I have presented in this book: self-responsibility, not blaming, compassion, empathy, learning by trial and error, patience, and the ninja use of exaggeration.

If you resist the urge to blow up a tense situation, and instead wait for a better option, it will come. It's not easy to endure pain, but a gentle touch helps. I was driving, so I could only reach over, hold Cheryl's hand, and contemplate. The better way appeared out of left field.

There is always something you can say or do that will make the best of a situation with your lover. Any tool in this book will point the way. If you memorize five of them, you will always know there is something you can do when the pressure is on. That is a delicious boost to confidence.

7

Additional Support for Skills

This book is based on the following premises:

- The sensation of sexual attraction is mediated by the brain's limbic system.
- The limbic system gives the signal for erectile tissue to fill with blood via the parasympathetic nervous system.
- The limbic system stores relationship stress and shuts down sexual attraction and erectile blood flow when stored stress reaches a critical level.
- Specific changes in behavior dial down stress and ratchet up safety. Sexual attraction then returns and the lock on erectile blood flow releases.

What sexual attraction leads to is up to the couple. It doesn't hurt to explore the infinite universe of sexual expression, through self study or classes. And sexual quality is a motivator. But this book is not a sex manual. Its purpose is the maintaining or rekindling of sexual *interest*. To get back to sex after moments when that seems impossible.

Transitioning difficult moments to something better is the gateway. You can facilitate those transitions if you are willing to learn by trial and error. You will err. You will think you are doing it right when you are not. Your lover's responses will be your teacher.

Here are some transitions that you may feel or observe:

- Tense to Calm
- Frustrated to Satisfied
- Confrontational to Cooperative
- Distant to Close
- Isolated to Connected
- Antagonizing to Supportive
- Critical to Appreciative
- Confused to Understood
- Resentful to Grateful
- Fearful to Trusting
- Angry to Sad
- Stressed to Hopeful
- Bored to Surprised
- Resentful to Excited
- Defensive to Apologetic
- Invalidating to Inquiring
- Shut Down to Turned On
- Repulsed to Attracted
- Wretched to Magical
- Attacking to Helping

It is not a lover's job to help with these transitions. They may resist. All you can do is try, and see what happens. Patience is useful since the seeds of transition can take a few minutes to sprout. The exact cause and effect might not be known. No worries. Just flow into the transition, if it happens, and be glad.

Pressure on your lover or yourself, to achieve a result, will backfire. Expectations are limitations. The higher your expectations, the more likely your lover will feel them. In my experience, the outcome is not predictable. Unpredictability makes lovers interesting.

Your lover is like a virtual-reality game programmed to defeat your sense of accomplishment. You start at level one, against a team of world-class programmers, who keep changing the rules. No other game comes close to this one's disregard for fairness. But something hooks you anyway. You hate the game at times, and swear to never play again. But you recover and give it another try.

Playing the game is the crucial part, rather than believing you can't. Everyone has to start at level one. There's no shame in it. No one is born a master. At first, you get clobbered. But over time, you can observe yourself progressing.

Frustration is frequent in the relating game. If there was an Xbox to smash, that might be cathartic, but destroying the console does not help you win. Attacking your lover does not help you win, either. Your lover is not to blame for your lack of success. Success will come through lessons learned.

You will go off track within seconds. But every direction that doesn't lead to a transition with your lover is a gift of information. You are not in control of that information. If the programmers are on, that information will short-circuit your bliss.

You will hope for success, but then nothing happens. Your lover doesn't melt into your arms. It may take time for your lover to lower their defenses against you. Your provoking habits have instilled caution.

You can't "make" a partner open up, and believe in a new you. They are convinced by your repeated actions. Everyone is a human being, and therefore autonomous. Unless you are in a consensual dom/sub relationship, you are not your lover's commander. Autonomy will always be a factor. Which is the case, even in elite military forces, according to Jocko Willink, author of *Extreme Ownership* and decorated Navy Seals commander in Iraq.

You will be amazed how quickly you revert to old patterns when your commands are not followed or hopes dashed. You will forget the new stuff you wanted to try.

Pause, or slow the interaction down to recognize what is going on inside you. The slower you go, the more likely you will notice an old pattern arise, so you can back away from it.

Discomfort will urge you to revert, so developing a new perspective on discomfort helps a lot. Try to think of emotional discomfort as merely a physical sensation. As with the plummeting temperatures of cold water plunging, you can train yourself to stay relaxed as relationship discomfort increases. The more relaxed your body is, the easier it is for blood to flow into your brain.

Since it is so easy for skills to evaporate under pressure, it's useful to phase them in by first practicing with yourself. Here is a possible phase-in:

Phase 1: Hack Yourself
Phase 2: Give Your Lover Feedback
Phase 3: Treat Your Lover Better
Phase 4: Cognitive Engagement
Phase 5: Emotional Engagement

Phase 1: Hack Yourself

Start right now hacking yourself. Go back to the list of provoking habits from Chapter 3. Try to notice when you are Criticizing, Judging, Ignoring, Blocking, Sidetracking, Invalidating, Analyzing, or Interrupting *Yourself*. Name the provocation to yourself, out loud, or at least silently.

The more challenging a situation is, the more likely a mental battle will occur. For example, you notice your lover has body odor, and are afraid to say something about it. You may fear hurting your lover's feelings.

Fear is the emotion of the moment, but shame might stop you from revealing your fear. The shame of fear is connected to many helpless moments in your past. That feels crappy, so a set of other thoughts comes to the fore, to lead you away from fear:

"He/she is the problem, not me." Defending

"Maybe the smell will go away." Ignoring.

"It's not nice to tell someone they smell." Judging.

"My nose is too sensitive." Criticizing.

"Maybe I didn't really smell something." Invalidating.

"I wonder why I smell this right now." Analyzing.

"Quit talking to yourself!" Blocking.

"I think that smells like garlic. Or maybe onion. Asparagus?" Sidetracking.

"Why is he/she making me smell this?" Taking Things Personally

One or all of these can freeze you into inaction. During this uncomfortable delay, unconscious signals betray that you are not enjoying the moment. The pressure is on.

Acknowledging the problem to yourself may give some relief.

"OK, I'm hoping the smell will go away. I'm ignoring myself. I'm ignoring how much impact the smell is having on my feelings toward my lover."

Going deeper within yourself is not without risk. You could get lost. But I feel the momentary dangers are worth long-term skill building. Not wanting to know about yourself may echo in not wanting to know about your lover. That would be fine, except your lover wants to be seen and heard.

What if you allowed yourself to feel the fear for a moment? That could cause a reaction in you. You might tremble or cower. That would be embarrassing, for sure. And that might be going too far. But such a reaction could happen if you let it. It is part of the real you.

Getting to the verge of an emotional reaction can help you take in the significance of what underlies your behavior. It could be a gentle exposure to a more in-depth self. Should this can of worms be opened? I believe it should, from a relationship standpoint. It allows for progress toward better relating skills. And, crucially, it reduces attacks.

You may say you keep your anger, depression, anxiety, or panic under control through discipline, or behavioral therapies. That's great. That helps you and your lover cope. But stuff can come up that blows past those techniques.

Control is useful but has its limits. It can dampen all expression and block informative discomfort. Discipline is useful for controlled exposure to issues, mimicking a successful treatment regimen for phobias. Thus you allow yourself to feel discomfort, contemplate it, and acknowledge the clearest cause and effect you can deduce.

For example, after some thought, you see yourself collapsing into helplessness every time something uncomfortable comes up with your partner. This visualization makes you so sad that you want to cry. Crying would be the perfect self expression, however, this example is limited to what you can achieve within your own mind.

You can self-soothe (talk to yourself): "That smells a bit strong right now, but I will probably switch to liking it in a few minutes when I am more aroused." Then do something arousing.

You can use pleasant body language: Move your nose to a smell you like and breathe it in. Focus on the pleasurable body sensations.

You can take an ego pause: "I suck at taking care of my needs," is the voice of ego you are familiar with. When you catch a deflating thought like that, you can offer yourself a re-frame. "A second ago I noticed I was uncomfortable with a smell. It will be interesting to see what I do about that."

You can recognize that you're taking it too personally: "Hmmm, I made myself angry when I thought my lover was being inconsiderate. The smell is accidental."

You can adjust your expectations: "I wanted to have sex, but now I can only think about my reaction to a smell. Sex would feel great, but learning how to handle a situation would feel good too." The blood vessels of sexual arousal open from relaxation and connection. The higher the expectations for sex are, the more likely stress will interfere.

You can identify the emotion you're feeling, moment by moment: "I was disgusted a moment ago. What am I feeling now?" The more relaxed you are, the more likely you will notice subtle changes in how you are feeling, and possibly zero in on pleasurable ones.

You can try to empathize with yourself: "Your efforts to handle this overwhelming smell are heroic!" Your empathetic mind might be so creative that you laugh out loud.

You can encourage yourself: "Great theory! There may be a link between smell sensitivity and seasonal allergies."

You can be vulnerable: "I didn't realize how deeply my reaction to specific smells affected my interest in sex."

You can apologize to yourself: "Sorry that I have a habit of not taking care of my needs. I'll find a better way."

You can learn by trial and error: "That was interesting. I wasn't able to adjust my expectations this time, but when I started breathing through my mouth and exhaling with sounds of pleasure, I forgot about the smell. I classify that as a successful transition, from stressed to hopeful." Successfully handling turmoil within your own mind can improve your expectations when facilitating your partner's struggles.

The self who wants to improve relationship interactions has to scrape off ad hoc coping strategies picked up earlier in life. That can be disorienting, but adding skills that offer many possibilities for transitioning touchy situations is worth upsetting the status quo.

Imagine that you believe this: "If I tell my lover about the smell, they will leave me." What happens if you find out this premise is untrue? Would you be giddy with relief? Or depressed, because your view of reality was inaccurate?

Giddiness, also known as happiness, tells you the answer. Analysis is not needed. You respond with joy, energy, and excitement to the new information. The content makes you smile. Your body perhaps gets sexually aroused.

Hacking yourself is tracking what gives you energy compared to what saps your energy, excluding food and drink. You should be able to feel the difference. That allows you to do something differently, no matter the situation.

Phase 2: Give Your Lover Feedback

When you give yourself space to explore, you may notice a disparity between self-treatment and the treatment you receive from your lover. You are not perfect, but you deserve encouragement, instead of derision.

Can you notice when you feel deflated, unhappy, stressed, anxious, afraid, or turned off during an interaction with your partner? Are you sometimes uplifted? Tune in to the fine details of time of onset, intensity, and duration.

You are responsible for your state of being. If you've dropped into a funk, that's on you, but you don't have to suffer. You can speak up about it if you choose.

You say, "I hate sushi!"

Your lover replies, "No, you don't!" It might be a small thing, but it feels weird in your gut. It feels like your lover incorrectly defined you, and that is irritating. You could strike back, or you could just say, "That felt invalidating. I prefer that you let me say what I feel in the moment, even if it's different from what I have said before."

If you did not give your lover permission to dump on you, providing feedback is a way to speak about your boundaries. Feedback is not your opportunity to dump back. It is a vulnerable reveal. The frame is: Lover said x, and I felt y; Lover did x, and I felt y. Feedback is restricted to what was said or done. It is not a commentary on character, only on how "I" felt. Felt means a feeling, an emotion.

"X makes me sad."

"I'm so happy about Z."

Not "I feel that you undersell yourself." That is not an "I" statement. That is a "you" statement.

Rephrased: "It makes me sad when you criticize yourself."

With more content: "When you said I should get a different job, I felt humiliated. I know I complain sometimes, but my job is fulfilling. I want to keep it. Can you help me with the hard parts?"

The primary purpose of giving your lover feedback is to hear yourself speak up for yourself. If your lover takes it in, apologizes, and changes behavior, then great. But don't expect it. Sharing your experience in a non-threatening way is the whole deal. It will have an effect even if you don't see it at first. But you will likely have to repeat the feedback. Sharing and repeating, sharing and repeating.

Feedback can be positive too. Thank and appreciate your lover for being supportive. It is in your lover's interest for you to be your best. Feedback helps your lover help you.

Phase 3: Treat Your Lover Better

The joy of treating yourself better, and asking for better treatment, builds in slack for a lover, as you contemplate treating them better.

Better treatment of your lover benefits *you*. You don't realize how damaging the provocations in Chapter 3 are. They turn off, take down, and destroy your partner, in the moment, and over time. Then they have less to give you.

Partners send you signals to stop provoking even though they try to keep up a brave front. But the brave front is counterproductive. It lengthens the time of exposure to hurts and deepens the cuts.

The hurts and cuts come back at you, no matter how hard your lover tries to control them. They don't know how to prevent hurts or heal them. What if you cut your lover with a knife, and those wounds didn't stop bleeding? Little cuts on the face, the neck, the shoulders, the belly, arms, and legs. Every day you would see them. Your lover tries to cover them up, but there are too many. You can always see them. Would seeing blood motivate you to stop cutting?

In the above analogy, blood symbolizes the wounding of spirit that results from being judged, criticized, ignored, rejected, and invalidated. The cut goes deeper, and the wound becomes more serious, for as long as the signal (bleeding) is not seen.

Your lover tries not to feel the cuts, but the pains add up. They affect performance (responses to you), like shin splints affect a gymnast's. At first, it's a slight limp, then crutches. Some injuries become chronic, forcing retirement (relationship breakup).

For most people, provoking behavior is a communication habit. That wouldn't hurt too badly if the habit stopped when the person got the signal. Not stopping is the problem. To your lover, not stopping feels like you don't care.

When you override your partner's signals to stop, whether through habit or need, you appear to be uncaring of the consequences. A lack of caring is felt as a lack of love.

He: "Look, I just bought some shampoo, since we are out."

She: "Thanks, but you'll have to take it back. I can see from the color on the label that it is not unscented."

He: "Fucking hell!"

The cursing outburst is a big dump of displeasure. She will feel like the target of that displeasure, and not look happy. In one second, He blew up. What will He do about it? Heightened arousal may make it difficult for him to apologize. More likely He will complain about their agreement to buy only unscented shampoo (blame Her), instead of taking responsibility for a minor mistake.

You may say "come on!" Stupid little outbursts are "just you." That they are normal. True. But that doesn't change their impact. There is a difference between spewing your shit and expressing your soul. Spewing is out of control and embarrassing. A soul expression feels powerful, makes you happy and proud. It makes you smile.

If you are not smiling, look within. It is time to consult the provocation list from Chapter 3. Try to notice sooner and sooner when you are provoking. Pay closer and closer attention to the effect you are having. How is your lover responding? Badly? Then stop.

Continuing the provocation makes it worse. It pushes your lover further away. Whatever message you want to deliver is lost. If you forget to stop, it is not too late. Stop when possible. Then apologize for the provocation that just occurred. Make it up, or start the interaction over. It's *never* too late to start over.

Once words have left your mouth, you have lost control over their power. You can't stop them from having their bloody effects. Remember, your lover has sensitivities. What you say and do brings them out. Imagine if every time you say the word "Go," your lover poops in their pants. Triggers are that wired in, and automatic. Less provoking = less partner triggering = better time for you both.

Monitor the volume of critical thoughts you have about your partner. Balance out negative thoughts with positive, unless you delight in self-torture.

It's not a lover's job to conform to your image of perfection. It wasn't their fault you fell in love. Perfection, after the dopamine spike diminishes, is just not out there. With practice, imperfections can turn into endearments. The emotional experience of connection can move your thoughts in that direction. It's all in your head, like Ecstasy. Make the best of it, or move on.

When you get annoyed, it is an opportunity to learn more about yourself. Your annoyance is your stuff. You can discipline yourself to not let that leak out through provocations, and to explore the underlying reasons for your annoyance.

It's in your hands. You can learn to pay attention to your lover's facial expressions, body language, words, and emotions. Is your lover enjoying the interaction with you? Playing with you, or fighting with you? The dynamic can change, from "how much of my pain can I dump on my lover?" to "how much encouragement and pleasure can I give my lover?"

The second one feels better unless you are a sadist. It feels better to see your lover smile, rather than frown, and know you affected that. It feels shitty to see yourself acting shitty.

Gaining control of provocations markedly improves your relating game score and opens up huge bonus point opportunities. Quality time together is foreplay.

Phase 4: Cognitive Engagement

As you dial down provocations, your lover may be more comfortable around you, and may even lower their guard. Thoughts and feelings held in check might see the light of day. That can mean more robust excitement, but also more fear, insecurity, and anxiety.

Lucky you. Now you get to be helpful. It only requires paying attention. Turn your body, face, and eyes toward your lover, and settle in for active listening. No action needs to be taken. Just observe, compassionately.

In this phase, you are emulating a science-fiction robot, whose field of vision is overlaid by a data scroll. On one side you see the list of provocations. On the other side, the list of disarming/connecting responses. You can see the text of your words on the overlay, classified as provocative or supportive, with proposed fixes for the provocations.

Fun, eh? Good observations lead to accurate computation and sensible output. A human brain's computational ability is compromised by emotions, however. As if the robot's AI lacked the computational power to interpret all the optical and auditory data.

Compromised computation turns the screen, the human mind, blank. The human freezes. Discomfort can lead the human to lash out. Bad design and programming can direct the robot to emit noxious gas or spray rubber bullets.

Lack of relating skill, or computational power, is a problem when the default response is harmful. A harmful response is out of proportion to the threat.

The body produces sensations. Interpreting those sensations is the dividing line. On one side is blaming your lover for your sensations. The other side is owning *all* of your sensations, soothing them, and making use of them.

Here is an example of two different computations:

"I'm so horny I want to lick you all over!"

"Ewwww, gross!"

Screen Scroll: Observation of defeated facial expression and posture.

My response was a childish judgment. Not the identity I want.

Can enthusiasm be recaptured?

"I'm so horny I want to lick you all over!"

Screen Scroll: Smile to indicate appreciation for the enthusiasm.

Not comfortable with the content, but like the enthusiasm.

What can I be enthusiastic about, or be a yes to?

Observe, respond, observe. If a provocation slips in, activating a corrective can fix it.

Male thought stream: She turned away five seconds ago. What did I say or do that might have caused that? Ah, right, I was critical. Apologize. Start over, or retract that content. Rephrase in a noncritical way. I felt x, when you y'd.

Female thought stream: I just sidetracked. He was talking about his day, and I had to put my two cents in about office politics. I made his story about me. Ooooops. Apologize and bring the conversation back to his day.

Encouraging the full bloom of story, content, and expression, wherever they go, feels like love. The attention-giver survives and benefits from a happier partner.

Your lover's expressions are like the inhabitants of a planet, and you are the Starfleet surface team. Your "prime directive" is to not interfere with their development path. The wily inhabitants have their agenda, which differs from yours.

The "away" team is under prepared, uninformed, unwelcome, and falls into a devious trap. But they don't give up. Even after a team member is killed, they try to accomplish their mission, and return to the ship.

The sudden urge to interfere (violate the prime directive) is *always* your shit. Can you control that reflex? For a few seconds? If things go well, you will get your turn. When it comes, your lover will be receptive, since you have not fired your Phaser.

You may be thinking, "What about spontaneity?" Spontaneity is great! The problem is the timeline. You want to paste your timeline into your lover's. But they don't sync, like a bad DJ transition. With better timing, your contribution, when it comes, relates to your lover's full expression, not a tiny piece.

Allowing your lover's full expression, in volume, or time, may affect your viewpoint, or change your story. You may resist that effect. But that effect is needed. It gets you updated.

A steady flow of updates, responses, and re-updates, keeping up with the truth of the moment, makes relationship life engaging. Genuine connection is similar to the pleasure of being high, instead of the pain of resentment, or dread.

A default of relaxed compassion helps your mind stay with the current moment, instead of veering off onto tangents. Even after listening for five minutes, or longer. What topic most synthesizes the last batch of content? Stay with the most salient topic, instead of sidetracking with scattershot topics that pop into your mind.

This default saves a *lot* of time and energy. You give the love (presence) needed. Done. Let go of content.

She: "I followed up on our conversation and got some polyisoprene condoms."

His face falls.

Scroll: I didn't expect that reaction. I'm disappointed that he's not happy. Did I do something wrong? No, this is not about me. The topic is his reaction. Is he feeling an emotion?

She: "You look sad."

He: "Yes, I suppose. When you told me about the condoms, I immediately thought about how tired I was, instead of being excited. That made me sad."

Scroll: Fuck! Here we go again. He's always got an excuse. Oooops. Provocation. Critical thoughts. Don't feel good. The topic is his sadness. What does sadness need? Comfort.

She moves in close to hug him sweetly. "Would you like to rest?"

He starts to cry. "No . . . Just shed a few tears. Your kindness has moved me from sadness to gratitude. Thank you, babe. You make me feel so good. Hmmmm. I'm starting to rise."

What if the word "you" is in the sentence? Doesn't that make it about you? Yes and no. You are a character in the play, but the topic is your lover's thoughts and feelings about your participation. Can you stay on topic?

She: "Whenever I hear her name, I think of your infidelity, and start to cry."

He: "I thought you were over that."

She (tearfully): "No."

He: "But you know what I was going through at the time. How long are you going to punish me?"

I hope by now it is obvious how much He made the moment about him, instead of about Her. No amount of avoidance, defense, or excuse helps a partner heal. How could it be different?

She: "Whenever I hear her name, I think of your infidelity, and start to cry."

He breathes to center himself and go deeper within. She is feeling emotion. Which emotion? He gently moves closer.

He: "You have spoken before about sadness over the loss of innocence."

She: "It seems like a bottomless well of sadness . . ."

He: "I am here for all of your sadness."

They both cry.

Dropping into compassion for Her, instead of the grip of guilt, created a focus on her deep sadness. Sadness filled all the space, crowding out the details of the past. He and She grieved together. The grieving is done when it is done. That crucial step cannot be skipped, if the relationship is to be renewed.

Phase 5: Emotional Engagement

Compassion is an excellent default, but it has a limit. That limit is a possible sense of separateness, caused by the concentrated effort of observing, updating, and monitoring provoking versus supportive responses. It can feel too controlled, contrived, one-sided, and denying of the desire to jump into the fire.

So is there a different way? Yes. Emotional Engagement. Letting in emotional expression, feeling it, matching it, being it. In a word, *empathy*. An empathetic response is a way to jump in.

But you said to control your urge to jump in. Yes! Glad you noticed. The difference is jumping in *with*, instead of *against*. Jumping in *with* your lover is welcomed. It is the ultimate form of being supportive and encouraging of full expression.

That is useful because fear of expression, displayed as cringing, or horror, feels like rejection to lovers. Rejection is a provocation and turns a potential deep connection into a disappointment, or depression, associated with you.

Empathy, on the other hand, creates a positive correlation with you. And is the cheapest possible response, in time, energy, and money. It's the ounce of prevention that mitigates a pound of cure.

No one in relationship can escape emotional engagement. Emotions happen within lovers, no matter how hard they try to suppress them. The most rational approach is to increase emotional abilities.

You probably like certain emotions, like happiness, and hate others, like sadness. This phase is about learning to love sadness as much as happiness. So your default response is not cringing in horror or scowling in disgust.

Fluency with all emotions is the ultimate fear remover. It allows you to handle any situation. Everyone needs to discharge emotional build ups. It is the relief, or healing, required. The problem is, most people cannot hear it at full volume. Or even at all. Their own bile rises up at the same time.

How can simultaneous spewing be avoided? With practice. Emotional fluency reduces urgency and builds in the understanding that you will get your turn. You can even get your turn right away, by allowing yourself to feel and express emotions in situations where there are minimal consequences, like watching a movie, or sitting in a parked car, or in a therapist's office.

Here are a set of frames that can create safety for exploring your own emotions, and potential engagement with your lover's emotions:

- Emotional expression is an artifact of the moment.
- It has no past or future meaning.
- Emotions are just a fraction of your whole identity.
- Useful emotional expression is a revealing of vulnerability in a safely held space.
- Emotional expression is a separate activity from commitment, agreement, planning, and negotiation.
- Start with the smallest possible situations and issues that need work.
- Schedule three times as much time as you might expect an engagement to take.
- Enter the engagement without expectations.

It will take more than a few practice sessions to gain proficiency at this. Let's imagine that your lover said "That shirt is dirty," and you said "OK," then went to change. You felt dejected, but didn't speak of it.

The next day, you notice the dejection from the night before is still there. Using the safety frames just described, a schedule check verifies you will be alone at home for another thirty minutes. You put your phone on Airplane Mode, decide this session will be five minutes long, and set a timer.

You are sitting at the dining table and feel like leaning forward to place your forehead on the table. Now what?

First minute: Many thoughts run through your head, and you forget what you are doing. A little discomfort from your forehead reminds you, so you sit up straight.

Next two minutes: You replay the shirt moment from the night before in your mind and notice that your mood turns gloomy with a tinge of dejection. Then you ask yourself why your lover's comment bothered you. The answers are self-critical, such as "I am absurdly sensitive!"

Last two minutes: Self-critical thoughts feel terrible, so you bring your mind back to neutral. The timer goes off, and you end the session.

Assessment: Was this an exercise in self-torture? It's a matter of perspective.

Negative Assessment: Reflecting on the shirt moment led to painful thoughts = more harm than good.

Positive Assessment: Reflecting on the shirt moment led to the awareness that certain situations with your lover cause an emotional reaction, which you suppress out of habit.

That's positive? Yes, because suppression is only partially successful. Dejection will return, in an ever larger number of situations, until that trigger is processed. I'm sorry to say that incidents with your lover that get you down have to be dealt with. Otherwise, a battery of resentment will charge up.

Resentment is a useful indicator of emotional health. It means that you have not taken proper care of yourself. That you have not spoken up for your needs powerfully enough. If *you* are not an advocate for your emotional health, then who will be?

You either manage your emotions, or they will run you. Honest reflection on your emotions helps to keep them more in their place as a *part* of your identity, instead of taking over your life during pressure-packed moments.

Specific times and places where you gift yourself emotional self-exploration, and even discharge, broadens your emotional experience base, so the steps leading up to a blowup, or attack, become more familiar. That familiarity gives you the opportunity to choose vulnerability in those moments, instead of anger.

The next "shirt" session might lead to new insights: "I feel embarrassed when They/He/She comments on the cleanliness of my clothes. It kills me when I am not perfect!" Eyes moisten as the next thought forms: "Why do I have to be so perfect?" This vein of exploration is huge.

Professional therapy can be very helpful, but there is no replacement for self-assessment and growth during situations that pop up real time. If you keep your eye out for it, an opportunity to drop into emotional vulnerability occurs "live," every day. Familiarity with these moments will make them less scary. The less afraid you are of your own emotions, the less afraid you will be of your partner's emotions. Emotional openness leads to connection, empathy, and sex.

Some male readers might object. "It seems like women lose respect for me when I express my emotions." But I think female reactions vary, depending on the situation. Straight women are turned off by male powerlessness, by men who can't face their fears. Trying and failing is admirable. That takes courage. Succumbing to fears leads to depression, which is not attractive.

A passionate expression, or emotional outburst, if appropriate to a situation, can be sexy. Crying with appreciation for a beautiful sunset, or with sadness over the loss of a friend, is the epitome of normal. If shame doesn't block vulnerable emotions, then such moments are fully lived by both partners.

Anger has its appropriate moments too. If one's spouse or children are attacked, a surge of angry energy may help with their defense. Anger may also be justified to re-establish boundaries, or enforce an agreement. But anger over one's own shame or embarrassment is different. Women are hard-wired to not be impressed by that.

For all genders, it is useful to notice when you have the impulse to say or do something, that in hindsight, is provoking. That impulse has a history. It was built by many unsatisfactory incidents from your recent or distant past.

Awareness and respect for the complete picture of your own emotional universe increases understanding of your partner's full set of shared and hidden expressions. That understanding feels like love, as if you were falling in love all over again.

29 Other Skill Development Steps

1. Broaden the range of emotions you can feel, in the most varied circumstances. Learn from each emotional cycle. Knowing what is happening to you is comforting. As time passes, you can more accurately predict the course that emotion will follow. Accurate prediction reduces fear.

2. Practice dropping into, and pulling out of an emotional state, in a series of short cycles. This exercise can help you view emotions more objectively. Tune in to the physical

sensations that each emotion creates. What positions does your body want to move into? Let your body move.

3. After you identify your lover's emotion, search for that emotion inside yourself.

4. Let yourself be turned on by your lover's "positive" states: happy, excited, sensual, sexy, joyful, playful, confident, courageous, and inspired. Those all feel good. Jumping into them can't hurt you. It's like slamming the books down and running out to the playground when the recess bell rings. If you are resistant, then why? Resentment is envy, jealousy, or a perceived imbalance.

5. Buy a book on improv, or take a class.

6. Exaggerate your natural responses, if they are in sync with your lover. Smile more broadly, laugh louder, be more shocked, and intensify your curiosity.

7. Take better care of yourself, so you will be less cranky. Increase the time you spend doing things that feel good, such as, yoga, meditation, exercise, hot tubs, and sex.

8. Practice body awareness. Notice more and more what sensations correlate with what moments. What makes your cheeks flush, jaws clench, or your guts tighten? What causes dissociation, or makes you feel self-conscious?

9. Start a breathing practice, either yogic or meditative, from a book or in class.

10. Pay more attention to your posture throughout the day. Change it up. Stretch and move more.

11. Notice how many negative thoughts you have about your partner. What effect do such thoughts have on your body?

12. Notice how often, and to what degree, you are afraid of your partner.

13. Look at guilt, shame, fear, or any other discomfort

related to your lover, as valuable information about yourself. Your emotional sensations of discomfort are within you. They are all about you, and not an attack by your lover.

14. Use a skill from this book to do something about your discomfort.

15. Increase ease with face-to-face interactions through Tantra exercises, from a book or in class.

16. Take yourself less seriously.

17. Empathy is not rational, or analytical. It requires a state change and therefore practice. Can you pick up a random object, like a rock, and care about it, or love it? How does that feel?

18. Do empathy as a practice, or discipline, even when you don't want to.

19. Let yourself feel your own emotions if they match your lover's—e.g., sad/sad.

20. Notice your lover's body language and facial expressions. Guess what they mean and sometimes ask for verification. Does your lover look comfortable around you?

21. Practice doing something positive for your partner, as a counter to critical thoughts or funky moods. Appreciate or acknowledge your partner.

22. Experiment with a tolerable level of exposure to your lover's discharges. By text? By phone on volume control? From the next room? In the same room, far apart? What boundary do you need to remain calm?

23. When your partner is angry, try to breathe deeply, and not take it personally. Consider safety precautions, but if anger gets to rage, it may subside on its own. Underneath the anger is hurt. Maybe it can be uncovered.

24. Use a timer to establish time boundaries that feel do-able if you want to practice skills with your lover. Even just a two-minute trade.

25. Notice how good a quality interaction with your partner feels.

26. During calm moments, experiment with discovering pleasure sensations anywhere within your body, without touching.

27. Notice the smallest things that are sexually arousing when you are with your partner, without shame or judgment. Enjoy and expand that arousal. Share your enjoyment with your partner if that feels safe.

28. Try to find where pleasure is hiding in every type of partner interaction. Pleasure in conversation, emotional sharing, and sensual touch.

29. Go to LoveandSexMastery.com to get a printable version of provoking behavior don'ts and connecting behavior dos.

If you are happy and have a perfect life, that is awesome. I am envious. If your relationship makes you feel like life is imperfect, it may not be that you have chosen the wrong partner. It could just be that each of you unintentionally pokes the other's bear. The skills in this book at least give you a chance to let the bears hibernate, and to have the most bountiful spring ever. That may not be enough. But you will feel better about yourself as a fully empowered lover.

8

Learning the Hard Way

How did I learn what to do when lovers attack? The hard way! My methodology came from learning how to turn my weaknesses into strengths.

A Pivotal Relationship

I married young and divorced after fourteen years. We were not well suited. Like a baby bird, I ventured out into the dating world. Luckily, I gobbled up better bedroom skills just in time for a fateful introduction to a hot therapist. We both felt a jolt of electricity when our hands met in greeting.

I fell for her and quickly got in over my head. I came to the relationship as a good lover, but that was about it. I had a problem with emotional discomfort. Difficult conversations wrecked my nervous system.

I was not prepared for life. I didn't get success genes; I was immature, introverted, insecure, self-conscious, and socially awkward. I had no chance with the popular girls. My brain went dead if attention turned in my direction, resulting in near constant shame.

Yoga, nature, sports, and sensuality were my refuge. Michele (not her real name) was into sex, but other than that, very different from me. She expressed her emotions and spoke her mind. Outside of therapy sessions, she had little concern for people's social and emotional sensitivities.

And I was the most sensitive person I knew. There was no part of me she couldn't challenge. Sex? How about three times a day? Each time special, romantic, and enhanced by fantasy or role-playing.

My contributions were slow to nonexistent. She wanted more. She wanted me to rise to her level of output. Pushing my hypoglycemic body is scary and painful, so I resisted, and I resented the pressure she put on me.

My frequent thoughts were: "You're stressing me out! I don't want to change! Get me out of here! Can't you see I am not comfortable! Why can't you just let me be? I can't do that! Can't you see that you're beating a dead horse?"

But she wanted what she wanted. And I stayed with her. Why? She was hot, intelligent, exciting, and I learned from the challenges. I knew I had to stop letting my physical and emotional liabilities define my existence and doom me to a life of misery.

One day I had a creative idea. I proposed a deal. If she took up rock climbing for me, I would try to learn counseling and emotional processing for her. She agreed, and we started climbing together. That was fun. After a few months, I hoped she would forget about my part of the bargain, but she did not.

Introduction to Counseling

With trepidation, I attended an RC (Re-evaluation Counseling) training. It was agony. Terror gripped me when it was my turn to reveal emotions. I admired the students who were vulnerable and emotional, but could not do it myself.

I survived enough training to enter the pool for peer counseling practice. In a one-on-one setting, I learned to be vulnerable. I discovered that revealing myself made me feel better. That expressing my pain reduced it.

But when it was my turn to fulfill the role of counselor, my mind locked on a single thought "What am I supposed to do?" Learning to get out of my self-centered head took many hours of practice, but I eventually transitioned from inadequate to competent. The secret I discovered was that clients wanted to express their feelings, and would, if I didn't interfere through my need to feel like I was doing something.

A client has to feel safe in order to discharge what they hold within. The "positive regard" vibe, expressed through body language and tone of voice, is comforting. That comfort continues if I keep my ego under control. By not running an agenda or any of the many intellectual and psychological theories I subscribe to.

I tell myself to "go in blank," so I can respond to *all* of a client's signals. So I am "present" with them, instead of absorbed with myself. Clients then feel I am *with* them, instead of observing from afar.

A space of non-judgment permits examination of inner truths. I have been fortunate to witness, countless times, the healing power of emboldened and empowered expression. That prepared me to work with sexuality-related issues that are so often a part of a client's difficulties.

Synchronistically, I stumbled upon an unconventional sexual healing and empowerment training that made a big difference in my personal life, and opened my eyes to the prevalence and intractability of sex-related difficulties within couples, individuals, and society.

Clients often believe something is wrong with them. That problems in their relationships have broken them and rendered them sexless. But, in the first session, we discover that their bodies are sexually responsive. The correct location of their problem is within their brain.

Their current or former partner or spouse lacked the skills I've described in this book, so the chances of the relationship vessel wrecking at sea were high. Reclaiming one's sexual empowerment is the life raft that enables renewed hope, survival, and purpose.

My Inner Baby Wants to Tantrum

My work has ingrained in me a clear understanding of what a helpful state is like. And makes the opposite of feeling helpful extremely obvious. When I get triggered, my compassionate robot-screen readout turns to hash. An ache in my guts is the only input.

The gaping chasm between how I feel in session and at good times with a lover, compared to times of conflict and triggering, is stark. I ask myself "what just happened?" and wait for an answer, as blankly as possible. Just feeling and observing. In this relationship circumstance, I feel that. Why? The answer boils down not immediately getting my way. When that occurs, I want to throw a tantrum. Like a baby.

Tantrum-throwing is like road rage. Some impediment

goes straight to blind anger. In my car, I curse, yell, and sometimes pound the dashboard. Cursing and pounding is a release. But it is only cathartic for a second because it doesn't express the underlying emotion, such as helplessness or feeling overwhelmed.

Rage is impotent. It does not affect the traffic jam. Traffic is impersonal. It hasn't targeted me. It isn't doing its clogging thing as a way to annoy me. When the road clears, I feel relief. That relief depends entirely on getting what I want.

A blowup with a lover is the same, except there is a witness. My lover's eyes on me force a sliver of self-observation. At that moment I feel crappy. I feel the sensations of a tantrum, and they are not good. My boiling brain wants to explode. My body spasms with frustration. I feel shame, disappointment, and failure. I chastise myself for, yet again, being incompetent.

I'm the opposite of happy-good flow in those moments. I'm the opposite of proud of myself. I lost control and went into full baby mode.

The Need for Self Reliance

But the world doesn't hear our squalling. It doesn't care about dashed hopes, wounded pride, searing shame, and pathetic whining. It demands self-reliance.

Competition rules nature, and human societies. Fulfilling needs and desires requires effort. Our genetic programming demands that we contribute to our tribe to receive its benefits. That trade-off eliminates guilt and boosts self-worth. The effort involved in contributing is worth it. We feel its reward every step of the way.

The pressure to fulfill our needs in the real world pushes

us toward a childish or adult response. Either way, the push can be resented. Our babies want to be given everything. The less our babies are given, the more they escalate their unhappiness.

An adult response is to accept the challenge and later get the benefit of feeling rewarded by accomplishment. Baby mode just can't grasp that. Baby mode is out of reality flow. In adult mode, I feel confident, in the game, able to function under pressure, and not tanked by opposition. Nothing is "wrong." And I can accept myself instead of being ashamed.

I can recognize my baby mode if I have the impulse to lie, avoid conflict, or deny responsibility. Or if I fear my partner. My baby wants to get away with something, instead of revealing a vulnerability. It only wants to escape long-term consequences. My baby hates revealing since that is an admittance of responsibility.

If I'm marginally functional, I allow myself a moment's baby-ness, with no expectation of getting ice cream. The point is to hear myself whine. I have let my baby express himself, so he knows he was heard and not ignored. So he's not covertly sucking his thumb.

Pouting and whining are at least steps toward revealing. They are an acknowledgment of pain. That helps to prevent pain from coming out in a poking manner. And appearing justified.

Staying with pain is the only way to go deeper. Into vulnerability. I understand the reluctance to be vulnerable. It can be scary. It can open you to self-criticism for weakness. That is a risk worth taking. I have found it almost always leads to things turning out better. Sharing is a sustainable authenticity and shame reducer. It lowers the burden of shit in the brain.

In my experience, hiding a weakness is more weakening

than revealing it. That's because it takes so much energy to keep the weakness separated from an intimate partner. Most likely that is a waste of energy since they already see it.

Acting out the childish self does not feel good. It does not feel successful and powerful. The childish self is easily hurt. Acknowledging that self is the first step to gaining control over its influence.

Acknowledging the baby means admitting that it affects behavior. Something is bothering me. I feel alone in my crib. It's painful to feel isolation in the company of friends and lovers. I wish they would rescue me. To have them all gather me in their arms and comfort me. To heal me forever.

Alas, no one notices. I have to take care of myself or ask for support. I want everything to be "great" in my world, so I deflate when it's not. It's not great when a crown falls off a tooth, a tire goes flat, or when a woman I'm attracted to comments on the sweaty smell of my shirt.

I was doing all right, then something deflating happens. I'm knocked out of flow. My internal logic board becomes overloaded with too many parallels to process. My functioning degrades. A sweet moment is in danger of turning sour.

The child self floats along in ignorance of the next challenge. When our lovers become their real selves, they are no longer programmed to please us. Hackers have taken over the holodeck. They give us discomfort instead of comfort, like a bad dream.

The Impulse to Blame

When a lover acts out or gives challenging feedback, it can be crushing. I still hate those moments, but I know they are not life-threatening. Like cuts and bruises sustained from a mountain bike crash.

Our thoughts about our injuries are the crucial thing. I'm not traumatized by a bike crash. I go out and ride a couple days later and have a great time. One can learn to recover from emotional pains the same way.

I have enough experience with the urge to fight, fly, or freeze that the process is no longer out of my control. I observe myself in freak-out and know that it's just a blip. I will return to normal. Sometimes quickly, if my partner assists.

I accept in my bones that I have chosen to be in relationship, no matter my mood or state of health. In preparation, I expand the net of my expectations to include more surprise, sadness, happiness, anger, disappointment, accomplishment, and craziness around me in every direction, like a blind aikido master attacked by seven swordsmen.

These perspectives keep my attitude towards my partner positive. If *you* are not feeling that way, something has thrown you off. The critical step is to look *within* for the problem, instead of assigning it to your lover.

Blaming a lover for our discomfort is the most significant problem lovers have with us. Especially if we act justified. When we deny that we are poking their bear. The bear doesn't like having its territory invaded.

Blame can come with a justification to punish. That might feel delicious, for a second. Until you register the negative/unhappy responses. It's happened before, yet you do it again. Only impulse control can intervene.

Increased self-awareness is the path toward controlling harm. Acknowledge to yourself the degree of childish impulse you feel, *every* time you have the urge to say something questionable.

The impulse might not be in words. You might feel like

throwing something. Or turning your back in disgust. Try to let in the most minute of these impulses. There's more underneath. Each one has meaning.

Dramatic thoughts pop into your head, reflecting emotions such as anger or sadness. Those moments are part of you, but not the complete you. Disturbing parts can lead you to the more comprehensive you. You can survive the crushing and return to life.

There is a place to assign blame for relationship suffering. It is life, parents, schools, culture, and bullies. Nature commands us to have sex and relationships but has not engineered us to do so well.

A Responsibility Principle

Our engineering is flawed and our preparation is haphazard, so we become dependent on a *fictional* lover. But a lover is no more able to hold us up than a cartoon cloud. At best, a lover is supportive. If you get that support, hallelujah! But you still have to work through your shit. It's falling through the cloud, either way.

Without falling, you can never have the pleasure of flying through the skies of relationship success. When you flap your wings, exercise your skills, and feel your confident self, you can be proud of yourself.

Depending on *yourself* for relationship success is empowering. And more reliable than depending on your partner. Self-reliance and creativity are far sexier than dependency and expectations.

Commitment to emotional maturity is not easy though. It requires some vulnerable shakiness on the way to sturdiness. The adrenaline boost of success is the reward for the risk of failure. It's just chemistry. Avoidance of all discomfort or responsibility is a downward spiral toward incapacity.

I still have to go through those crushed-to-confident cycles. I'm still embarrassed by my inner baby. But I can now sometimes have fun with it. If I'm feeling light enough, I can pretend I am an actual baby for a moment, in a pouting and whining improv. That is a way for me to discharge my feelings. It can be cathartic and even funny.

Whichever way I manage it, taking 100 percent responsibility for all of my emotional discomforts is the most empowering principle I have discovered. This principle allows me to give maximum slack to my partner. In the depths of understanding myself, I can understand her. I can understand her struggles, trials, and errors. So I can reward her when she tries her best, instead of punishing her when she is less than her best.

Most couples are not aware of or cannot put into practice this principle. The result is mutual blame, and resulting clenched jaws, blank stares, and urges to attack.

Updating Reality

Happiness does not return without effort. One partner has to, or both partners have to, do things differently. To stop poking, to listen and see.

It takes time to see each other anew. Time for curious thoughts to replace critical ones. Enough time for partners to understand each other. To understand, they have to jettison habitual responses.

I know how hard it is to release cherished, sacred blame. But not releasing it guarantees relationship destruction. Blame is poison. Curiosity is the antidote. Curiosity and non-judgment give life instead of taking it. So the inner child can recognize itself and see the possibility of emotional maturity. So it can deal with reality.

Conflict increases as lovers' realities diverge. I learned that syncing up is not as traumatic as I'd expected. A lover saying "I want all of our sex to be romantic" doesn't mean that literally. It's only the first step toward an amazing possibility. Toward a blending of the real her and the real me.

The real me and the real her can negotiate. Negotiation is the end game since it isn't win/lose. It considers the needs of both parties. The adult, unashamed of its needs, can negotiate a successful agreement. Then an improved life goes on. Without the fear of an angry bear.

Choosing Sex

Conflict is possible wherever differences exist between lovers. That is the realm of negotiation. But certain conditions are inherently favorable, such as safety, ease, pleasure and sex.

This book is designed for lovers who wish for a favorable relationship and want to have sex, or at least some form of sexual contact. Limbic systems at ease are highly adaptable. Hence, a final story.

Cheryl's default mode is readiness for sensual touch, but when she's hungry, nothing gets between her and her food. One evening, Cheryl prepared a delicious Middle Eastern chicken dish and was waiting for my return from a mountain bike ride. We had casually agreed to pop into the hot tub at six, before eating. Cheryl normally eats earlier than that, so by six she was starving.

I arrived in the kitchen at 6:05. Between 6 and 6:05,

Cheryl lost patience. She greeted me with an exasperated sigh, so I offered to eat dinner with her right away. But no, she wanted to follow through with the tub plan.

We got into the tub, at opposite sides. Cheryl's face was serious and tense. On top of a delayed dinnertime, her work day was topped off with a vigorous hip hop dance class. She was well beyond her recovery needs.

I relaxed and felt the water's heat for a minute, but couldn't get into pleasure. An insecure thought distracted me: "How much am I to blame for Cheryl's unhappy state?"

Such thoughts were a rabbit hole I could not get out of in my past. Even now, my first response is to "take it personally" whenever a lover appears less than happy. I freeze in a matching unhappiness.

But I thaw quickly. My morose wallowing sets off an internal alarm bell. That alarm reminds me to do something. To initiate a change of state.

I moved forward, reached down to one of Cheryl's calves, and massaged it. As I gently worked both legs, Cheryl slid lower into the water, leaned her head back on the tub frame, and sighed with pleasure as her face lit in a wide grin.

That was encouraging, so I moved my fingers to one foot, pulled it just above the water, and began to suck her toes. I rarely suck on toes, but the idea spontaneously entered my mind.

Cheryl's sounds of pleasure increased. I love sexual responsiveness and got hard from her enjoyment. We always tub naked, so when Cheryl looked up, she could see my fullness. The twinkle in her eyes filled the sky as she glided across the tub and got on top of me.

That "Wretched to Magical" transition was healing for us both. We have found that difficult mental or emotional states can release their grip, and physical pains can be forgotten.

That is the power of shamelessly welcoming the gift of pleasure.

Giving or receiving pleasure is not a frivolity. Sex and relationship expert, Esther Perel, shared her unique view of the importance of pleasure during a February 14, 2013, TED Talk. Esther grew up in a community of Holocaust survivors, and in her observation there were two groups: "Those that didn't die, and those that came back to life."

Those who didn't die could not feel pleasure, and were consumed by anxiety. "Those that came back to life understood the erotic as an antidote to death."

The average human does not face death every day, but partnered individuals face the death of their relationships. Both partners participate in the kill. Each carries legacy behaviors that trigger the other. The specter of shut down is inescapable, but the shadow side of intimacy can be faced.

I've trained myself to take action as soon as it appears that Cheryl is struggling. Delaying only lengthens suffering. But sometimes I'm the miserable one. When I'm sullen and withdrawn, often correlated with hypoglycemia, Cheryl takes command. Her talented ministrations of cooing touch take about five minutes to overcome my body's blood chemistry resistance.

That welcome shift arrives with a bonus: My favorite sexual interludes now happen when I start out feeling crappy. I have learned not to fear my biologically induced downers. If I can't soothe myself, I trust that Cheryl can.

Someone needs to know when and how to take action. You either take favorable action, or a non-favorable action will be taken for you. You are always either choosing the path of sex, or not. Choosing is in *your* head.

I have learned to dump the shit in my head that interferes with giving or receiving, as soon as possible. That simple discipline has melted into Cheryl a positive sexual response to me. And she has laid in my tracks to her. Our pathways to pleasure and ease are primed.

Cultivating an attraction pathway takes a little time and effort every day. Funny thing though, there is nothing better to do with a lover. And realistically, nothing is easier.

This book provides methodologies for handling many types of relationship challenges. Like whipping out a 14-in-1 multi-tool. But it's also nice to have a garage full of tools for specific applications. Stay tuned for future books that will detail my perspectives on sexual healing, sexual performance, and emotional competency.

The list of things that mess with lovers is long.

Postscript

I believe the relationship principles in this book to be widely applicable. If you agree, consider leaving an online review.

My coaching website is LoveandSexMastery.com.

My author website is SevaKenn.com.

Bibliography

Authors, Contributing. "Emotional Contagion." Wikipedia, Wikimedia Foundation, accessed January 15, 2018, en.wikipedia.org/wiki/Emotional_contagion.

Authors, Contributing. "Empathy." Wikipedia, Wikimedia Foundation, accessed January 15, 2018, en.wikipedia.org/wiki/Empathy.

Authors, Contributing. "Limbic system." Wikipedia, Wikimedia Foundation, accessed May 22nd, 2018, en.wikipedia.org/wiki/Limbic_system.

Authors, Contributing. "Mirror Neuron." Wikipedia, Wikimedia Foundation, accessed January 15, 2018, en.wikipedia.org/wiki/Mirror_neuron.

Barrett, Lisa Feldman. *How Emotions Are Made: The Secret Life of the Brain.* New York: Houghton Mifflin Harcourt, 2017.

Bloom, Paul. "Against Empathy." *Boston Review*, October 24, 2016. bostonreview.net/forum/paul-bloom-against-empathy.

Campbell, Susan M. *Getting Real: The Ten Truth Skills You Need to Live an Authentic Life.* San Francisco: New World Library, 2001.

Cook, Gareth. "How the Power of Expectations Can Allow

You to 'Bend Reality.'" *Scientific American*, October 16, 2012. www.scientificamerican.com/article/how-the-power-of-expectations-can-allow-you-to-bend-reality/.

Darwin, Charles, et al. *The Expression of the Emotions in Man and Animals*. New York: Penguin Books, 2009.

Fairbanks, Eve. "Love in the Age of Big Data." *Huffington Post*, 2015. highline.huffingtonpost.com/articles/en/love-in-the-age-of-big-data/.

Harris, Sam. *Waking Up: A Guide to Spirituality without Religion*. New York: Simon & Schuster, 2015.

Jackins, Harvey. *Fundamentals of Co-Counseling Manual (Elementary Counselors Manual) for Beginning Classes in Re-Evaluation Counseling*. Seattle: Rational Island Publishers, 1982.

Jackins, Harvey. *The Human Side of Human Beings: The Theory of Re-Evaluation Counseling*. Seattle: Rational Island Publishers, 1978.

Katie, Byron, and Stephen Mitchell. *Loving What Is: Four Questions That Can Change Your Life*. New York: Three Rivers Press, 2003.

Kuchinskas, Susan. *The Chemistry of Connection: How the Oxytocin Response Can Help You Find Trust, Intimacy, and Love*. Oakland: New Harbinger Publications, 2009.

Lowen, Alexander. *Bioenergetics*. New York: Penguin Books, 1976.

Mariotti, Agnese. *The Effects of Chronic Stress on Health: New Insights into the Molecular Mechanisms of Brain-Body Communication*. Future Science OA, November 2015. www.ncbi.nlm.nih.gov/pmc/articles/PMC5137920/.

Morgan, John, and Jennifer Tzar. *"Peyote on the Brain."* *Discover*, February 1, 2003. discovermagazine.com/2003/feb/featpeyote/.

Navarro, Joe, and Marvin Karlins. *What Every BODY Is Saying: An Ex–FBI Agent's Guide to Speed-Reading People*. New York: Harper Collins, 2015.

Nicastro, Dr. Rich. "Relationship Help: Understanding Your Emotional Triggers." Strengthenyourrelationship.com, January 3, 2012. www.strengthenyourrelationship.com/relationship-help-understanding-your-emotional-triggers/.

Obringer, Lee Ann. "How Love Works." HowStuffWorks, February 12, 2005. people.howstuffworks.com/love7.htm.

Perel, Esther. "The secret to desire in a long-term relationship". YouTube video, 19:10. Posted [February 2013]. https://www.youtube.com/watch?v=saoRUmGTCYY.

Rosenberg, Marshall. *Nonviolent Communication: A Language of Life; 2nd Edition*. Encinitas: Puddledancer Press, 2003.

Sapolsky, Robert M. *Behave: The Biology of Humans at our Best and Worst*. New York: Penguin Press, 2017.

Schnarch, David Morris. *Passionate Marriage: Keeping Love and Intimacy Alive in Committed Relationships*. New York: Holt Paperbacks, 1998.

Skomorowsky, Anne. "How Molly Works in the Brain." *Scientific American*, March 10, 2015. www.scientificamerican.com/article/how-molly-works-in-the-brain/.

Waal, F. B. M. de. *The Age of Empathy: Nature's Lessons for a Kinder Society*. New York: Harmony Books, 2009.

Willink, Jocko. "Discipline Equals Freedom Podcast." *The Tim Ferriss Show #187: Jocko Willink on Discipline, Leadership, and Overcoming Doubt*. Podcasts.com, October 20, 2017. www.podcasts.com/the-tim-ferriss-show/episode/187-jocko-willink-on-discipline-leadership-and-overcoming-doubt.

Woolfe, Sam. "Is DMT Really Produced in the Pineal Gland?" Samwoolfe.com, January 11, 2018. www.samwoolfe.com/2017/09/is-dmt-really-produced-in-pineal-gland.html.

.

Made in the USA
Middletown, DE
19 February 2020

84959060R00110